Y0-BDO-768

Orchard Lake Road
Farmington Hills, MI 48018

PHOENIX COUNTRY

Edited by Nigel Gray

Thomas Billhardt
Robert Bly
David Craig
Lawrence Ferlinghetti
John Gerassi
Nigel Gray
Philip Jones Griffiths
Nam Ha
Nhat Hanh
David Harris
To Huu
Ron Kovic
Denise Levertov

Ewan MacColl
Adrian Mitchell
Giang Nam
Tim O'Brien
John Sack
Nguyen Sang
Pete Seeger
Ken Sprague
Goran Sonnevi
Nguyen Trung Thanh
Nicholas Tomalin
Kurt Vonnegut

The Journeyman Press
London & West Nyack

PL
4378.9
.P6
1980

OR 5/81

First published as a *Fireweed* Special Issue, 1976
Reissued by the Journeyman Press, 1980
97 Ferme Park Road, Crouch End, London N8 9SA
and 17 Old Mill Road, West Nyack, NY 10994, USA

ISBN 0 904526 58 5

Acknowledgements remain
due to all those who helped to produce
the first edition of *Phoenix Country*; also to
the following publishers: *Esquire Magazine* for
M by John Sack; Andre Deutsch and the *Sunday
Times* for *The General Goes Zapping Charlie Cong* by
Nicholas Tomalin; *Redbook Magazine* for *Where
Have You Gone, Charming Billy?* by Tim O'Brien;
City Lights and *Stand* for *The Teeth Mother Naked At
Last* by Robert Bly; Essex Music for the songs by
Pete Seeger; *Rolling Stone* for the article by David
Harris and Ron Kovic; and Medical Aid for
Vietnam and The British Hospital for
Vietnam for some of the photographs.

Printed in Great Britain

Contents

The Ivory Comb
Nguyen Sang

The relay post was a little house somewhere about the middle of the Plain of Rushes, situated in a forest of myrtles.

That night of bright moonlight there were many people waiting inside. The water had already risen all round the post while we had been waiting for the boat to come and take us on the next stage of our journey.

Not knowing quite how to pass the time, we had nothing to do but stretch our limbs and relax our cramped legs.

Among us there was an old comrade who knew a lot of good stories, especially stories about the war of Resistance.

Usually when he was about to begin a story there would appear on his lips a particularly seductive and mischievious smile. This time, however, his expression was different. He seemed to want to begin, but instead of starting off he remained quite still, without speaking, his head slightly on one side as though absorbed in thought.

It appeared he must be meditating something serious.

Outside the wind was getting up and the waves were crashing against the trunks of the trees. The little house began to pitch and toss like a boat.

Some herons had woken up and were flapping restlessly in the tops of the trees.

It seemed the wind and the waves were beginning to produce some disturbing effect in the memory of the old man. He held his head as though listening and then began his story in a low voice, sometimes resting his far away look on the waves, sometimes on the horizon or on the faint stars.

I am going to tell you of something that happened already more than a year ago but every time I think about it I still feel troubled and sad.

I was making a transit between two relay posts — MG to DA. When the motor canoe arrived everyone was anxious to know who was in charge. This wasn't simply curiosity. We needed to know because the head of the relay station had warned us that this stage of the journey would be long and dangerous.

"The first part of the stage will be made in canoes and there will be a risk of helicopters. The second will be on foot and you could meet with an ambush. In the case of helicopters stay calm, don't get agitated, don't start doing anything, but wait for the orders of your guide."

In other words we were to confide ourselves entirely to whoever was in charge of the party. For this reason it was very natural I should be anxious to see this person in whose hands I was about to place my destiny. But it was already dark and from all I could make out, there seemed to be no one but a slender young girl wearing, with a casual air, an American carbine in a bandolier and a kerchief over her head.

I remembered having heard it said that there was somewhere on this route a young and very bright girl comrade. It was told of this girl that upon one occasion while she was conducting a party of travellers, as the party approached a river crossing-point she abandoned them in the rear while she went with another comrade to explore the shores. When they had reached an orchard by the edge of the water, she realised that they had got themselves into an ambush. Without losing her nerve she at once called her companion loudly enough to make sure she could be heard by the enemy. "Right. All clear. You can fetch the others. I'll cross the river and bring the canoes." These words had a prearranged meaning. Her companion doubled back on their tracks and conducted the travellers by another route so that they could cross the river at a point several kilometers distant.

As for the girl, before getting into the river she paused for a moment to place a couple of grenades. She escaped from the adventure without a scratch. The enemy never moved, thinking they were about to grab a whole party. After a long pause, seeing nothing coming their way, the mercenaries realised they had been tricked. They emerged and could only vent their anger by cursing and swearing, after which they began to beat a retreat. At this point they passed where the grenades were waiting for them. Several of them were killed.

When they told this story people would add that this girl had an exceptional instinct. She could locate the enemy at great distance and even distinguish between the Yankees and their Vietnamese puppets.

I considered that if it should happen that she was to be the one to conduct our canoe we had not too much cause for anxiety.

"How many women are there working in this station?" I asked the girl.

"Two of us," she replied. "A comrade who does the cooking and me."

So it must be she indeed, and I felt a kind of elation. From her voice I judged her eighteen or at most twenty.

Feeling strongly moved by sympathy towards her I would gladly have continued the conversation, but I held my peace seeing her busily engaged in coiling the mooring rope. She stood up a moment later and turned towards the second boat.

"Right . . . . . Do I go first?"

The comrades in the other boat replied—

"You first elder sister."

"Good luck, youngest sister."

"What is the meaning of that?" I wondered. "One lot calls her elder sister and for the others she is youngest sister." She hailed them with a touch of mischief, calling them her "little brothers", then turning back to her travelling party she addressed us with more respect.

"Uncles and older brothers, if you have any things of special importance on you it would be best if you could put them in your pocket or in a separate little bag in case we meet with helicopters or an ambush." She warned us of accidents we might encounter, but in a gentle voice, quite different from the severe tone of the commander of the station.

Then she got the engine started. The canoe chugged off, detaching itself from the tuft of trees, and took the lead. The river wind refreshed us deeply, everyone felt lighter at heart. Acting on the recommendations of our guide, people started fumbling in their luggage. My papers and money for the journey were already in my pocket. What else was there that I had to take special care of? I suddenly remembered a little ivory comb and at once began to search for it in my travelling sack. I put it in my little satchel with my papers, then hugged it against my heart in an interior pocket which I carefully secured with a pin. I never could look at that comb without emotion.

It was in the first days after the armistice of 1954 that I went back to visit my village with a friend called Sau. Our houses were side by side on the bank of a little canal that flows into the Mekong. We had left together to join the Resistance at the beginning of 1946 at the time when our province was invaded by the French. Sau left behind his wife and their baby, a little girl less than a year old.

During the war of resistance Sau's wife found it possible to visit her husband several times. He always implored her to bring the child with her, but the journeys through the battlefields of the West were difficult and she didn't dare take her little girl through the jungles. Her objections were reasonable and Sau couldn't find it in his heart to reproach her.

During these eight long years of struggle he never saw his daughter except in one photograph. When at last it was possible to go back home to his village this father's heart was excited to bursting.

As our canoe touched land we saw a child of about eight with short hair cut just below the ears, dressed in black pantaloons and a pink shirt, playing under the mango trees in the courtyard of his house. Certain that this must be his daughter, Sau leapt to the bank and strode thoughtlessly towards the child, crying:

"Thu, my baby!"

No doubt he imagined his daughter would fling herself into his arms. He held his arms wide as he advanced, but at the sound of his voice the child had jumped away and stood looking at him with huge eyes. The father couldn't contain his emotion. Now, whenever he was under emotional stress the long scar which had been ploughed across his right cheek by a bullet turned red, stood out and became dreadful to look at.

He moved forward, step by step, his open hands held forward, repeating in a trembling voice:

"It is me, your daddy, my little one. It is me, your daddy . . ."

The little girl looked at him with a defiant expression, blinking her eyelids with bewilderment. The suddenly she turned pale and ran away crying, "Mummy! Mummy!"

Sau remained, following her only with his eyes, his face sombre and his arms hanging as though they had been broken.

As the road was long that we had to travel at that time we could only stay three days at home. In this short time the little girl refused to acknowledge her father. She would not allow him near her. The more tenderly he tried to win her favour the more she rejected him. He wanted to hear her say "Daddy" but this she obstinately refused. Once when her mother asked her to tell Daddy to come for a meal, she replied, "No, Mummy, you tell him yourself." The mother lost patience and threatened the child with a kitchen stick. Obliged to obey, the child proceeded to shout, as though to nobody in particular, "Come to dinner! Come to dinner!"

Sau pretended not to hear, hoping that she would say "Daddy, come to dinner", but the little girl remained in the kitchen shouting, "Rice is ready."

Sau didn't move, he heard the little girl declare to her Mama, rather crossly, "I called, but *they* don't want to hear me."

At this point Sau turned round, looked at her with a smile, shaking his head. He couldn't speak, nor even weep. He felt suffocated with sadness.

Another time when the mother had to go out to buy food, she told her daughter that if she needed anything she would have to ask her Daddy. The little girl didn't say anything and stayed alone in the kitchen. Hearing the rice boiling, she lifted the cover to let out the steam. Some water needed to be taken out, but as the pot was too big for her to lift, the child turned her eyes furtively towards Sau.

I wondered at this point how she would deal with this situation. Surely she would have to ask her father for help. After looking round about, desperately, for a moment, she called out: "The rice has boiled enough. Some water needs to come out."

She still spoke as though to nobody in particular, so I suggested to her, "You should say, 'Daddy, please pour out some water for me'."

She pretended not to hear and again insisted, to no-one in particular, "The rice has boiled enough. It will get all gluey."

Sau did not move. I said to the child, "If the rice is getting gluey, you'll get a row from your Mother. Why don't you ask Daddy? Can't you say 'Daddy' — is that it?' "

The pot bubbled more and more menacingly and seemed on the point of boiling over. The little girl began to be afraid. She hung her head doubtfully, but she wasn't going to be beaten. She took a cloth to lift the pot, but couldn't manage it. She looked about her. The furious bubbling of the water demanded attention. She looked at the rice, made a face at it, then calculatingly peeped at us. Seeing her in such a fix I was torn between compassion and the need to laugh, thinking she would be bound to give in. But suddenly she had an idea, raised herself on her tiptoes to get a spoon and proceeded to remove the water very carefully a spoonful at a time, muttering to herself as she did so, heaven knows what.

A tough character!

During the meal that day Sau put into his daughter's rice bowl a treat, a little handful of fish roes. She dug her chopsticks into the bowl, then with a swift movement flung the eggs onto the floor, and then replaced what remained of her rice on the serving dish. Beside himself, Sau fetched her a whack on the behind, crying out, "Oh, why are you so obstinate?"

I thought she would have cried, rolled on the floor, upset the bowl or run out. But she remained silent, her head bent low. Then, she scooped up the lump of fish-eggs from the floor with her chopsticks and put it back in the bowl and went out. When she got to the water's edge, she jumped into the boat, undid the chain with a great rattling and banging and shoved herself across the canal. She went to her grandmother — her mother's mother, and remained there crying. In the evening her mother went to look for her, but couldn't persuade her to return. Sau was due to go away again the next morning, but his wife was reluctant to force the little girl to come home.

The next morning all the friends and relations crowded around. The child was also there with her grandmother.

Sau, occupied with all these people, made no sign of recognition towards his daughter. His wife meanwhile was busying herself with preparing his travelling gear, filling his satchel with all kinds of necessities. The little girl, left to herself, retired into a corner or hung about by the door, looking at all the visitors gathered around her father. She no longer wore that obstinate and defiant expression, but seemed sad. Her long eyelashes lowered made her eyes look very large. The fierce look they had shown for the past few days had given place to a brooding and thoughtful air.

When the time came to say the goodbyes, having shaken hands with everyone, Sau searched with his eyes for his daughter and saw her sitting apart in a corner. No doubt he wanted to embrace her but he seemed afraid to see her resisting and running away from him again, so he only looked at her with an expression at once sad and full of tenderness. I saw the big eyes of the child suddenly become troubled.

"Come now. Daddy is going away, my child," Sau whispered.

We all, as indeed he himself, expected her to remain rooted to the spot, without showing any response. But quite unexpectedly she cried out at the top of her voice.

"Daddy! Daddy!"

It was a burning cry. It seemed to tear through the silence and pierce the heart of everyone present. It was the cry that she had held within herself for long years, which burst out now unbearably. She cried as she ran to him and quick as a squirrel leapt at her father.

She held him with all her strength, sobbing, "Daddy! I won't let you go. Stay at home with me."

Her father took her in his arms. She hugged and kissed his hair, his neck, his shoulders and the long scar upon his cheek . . . .

It was in this way, her Grandmother told me afterwards, that she had at last discovered the evening before why the child had refused to know her father.

She had put the question to her, "Why do you refuse to be nice to him?" adding, "He is, after all, your father."

"It can't be true," the child declared, jumping on her bed.

"How can you say it's not true. The fact is that your Daddy has been away a long time and you have forgotten him."

"But this person doesn't look like the photograph taken of Daddy and Mummy."

"Of course not. During all this time Daddy has got a bit older, that's all."

"Oh, it's not that. Daddy never had such an ugly thing on his cheek."

So that was it! The grandmother heaved a long sigh. She explained that her Daddy had been wounded in a fight against the French. She reminded her of the crimes done by these people at the mouth of the Canal where they had had a military post. The child listened in silence. She turned over in her bed and from time to time a grown-up sounding sigh escaped her. The next morning she asked her grandmother to take her home. She had come to understand her father now that it was time for him to go.

So she clung firmly to her father, clasping him in her arms. Not wishing her to see that he was crying, Sau fumbled for his handkerchief to dry his tears, then stroking her hair, he said to her, "I am going now, my little one, but I shall come back to live with you."

"No!" she cried, clinging with all her might round his neck, and as though her arms were not enough to hold him, she used her legs as well, while her shoulders shook with the violence of her emotion. People who saw this scene were so moved by it that many could not hold back their tears. As for me, I felt almost choked. I even thought to propose to Sau that he should stay a few more days. But this presented problems. We didn't know if we were required for regrouping in the North. It was absolutely necessary that we should be there on the day appointed to receive orders and hold ourselves in readiness. So we really had to go.

The neighbours surrounded the little girl to console her. Her mother said to her, "Thu, my little one, let him go. When our country is united again he will come back to live with us."

The grandmother stroked her hair.

"My little granddaughter is a clever one. She must let Daddy go, and when he comes back he will buy her a beautiful comb for her hair."

The child cuddled her father, saying between sobs, "When you come home you will buy a comb for my hair, will you Daddy?" And she allowed herself to slide slowly to the ground.

Well, we had to return to the Western theatre of the struggle. We were not included in the lists for military regrouping.

The years '54 to '59 were hard, as we all know. The American-supported administration of Diem hunted out and persecuted with great savagery the old fighters of the Resistance. We had to take refuge in the Jungles. About the life we led in those days I could tell stories for days on end. Some nights we would find ourselves surrounded by enemy commandos as often as three times in succession. It sometimes happened that we were reduced to eating leaves instead of rice. But to return to the story of my friend and his little daughter—

At night in the forest, lying in his hammock under a nylon net, Sau thought of his child with remorse for having once hit her.

One day when we had been thinking aloud together in low voices, he got up suddenly.

"The moment has come. People hunt elephants in this part of the forest. I must make an ivory comb for my little girl." He began after that to look for the opportunity to get a piece of ivory.

8

Then a good chance came his way. In order to supplement our diet, our group decided to organise a big hunt, not with guns, but with poisoned arrows, for it was essential to preserve silence in the jungle. The hunters had no intention of killing an elephant, but it happened by chance that they found themselves near one. Some of them would have spared it, but Sau decided he had to get it. With a friend he hid himself in a thicket, and when the animal came along trampling the vegetation, they sent two arrows into its eyes.

I remember that evening. It was after a day of rain in the forest. The leaves of the trees still held so much water that the whole forest sparkled. I was working under my canopy when I suddenly heard a shout. Along a path leading from the depths of the forest Sau came running, panting and brandishing in his fist a piece of ivory. He was as delighted as a child. He found a shot-out American 22mm cartridge, flattened it and made a little saw, with which he sliced the piece of ivory into thin sections.

In his leisure moments he occupied himself with carving the teeth of the comb, one by one with his saw.

This work he did with the greatest care in the minutest detail, like a goldsmith.

I loved to watch him. I don't know why. I felt happy to see the ivory dust falling softly around his feet.

Every day he managed to carve a few more teeth of the comb and soon it was finished. It was a little more than six centimetres long and one and a half centimetres wide, a comb fit for a young girl, with well-spaced teeth for controlling a wealth of long hair.

On the back were a few words which Sau had patiently engraved.

"To my daughter, Thu.
          Affectionately, Daddy."

Without having passed through the hair of his daughter this ivory comb had nevertheless served to smooth out some of the tangles in the father's heart. At night when he was thinking of his daughter he would take it and pass it through his own hair to give it a fine polish. Looking at it made him yearn more than ever to see his child again.

But misfortune intervened. One day in the end of the year 1958 (at this time we had not renewed our armed resistance) Sau fell victim to a great "mopping up operation" put on by the Diemist regime supported by the Americans. A Yankee machine gun bullet from an aircraft pierced him in the chest. In his last moments he took the comb from his pocket and gave it to me with eyes fixed on me in a long look. I do not know how I could describe that look, but it still often happens to me that I see again in my mind the eyes of Sau.

"I will see that the child gets the comb you've made for her," I whispered.

At that he quite simply shut his eyes and died.

Comrades, in this dark time we had to live furtively. It was also necessary to die furtively. It was not possible to raise a memorial mound for Sau, for if the enemy had found it, they would have dug him up and followed us. The grave, therefore, was soon lost in the floor of the forest. All I could do was to make a cut in the bark of a tree to mark the place.

That was how we had to live and die. Who could bear such an existence . . . .?

So we were forced to take up arms again. When we were established in a well-defended base I was visited there by a relative from our village. I wanted to give the comb for Thu to him, but he told me that Madame Sau and her daughter were no longer in the village.

After the various operations by the Americans and their puppets, the "denunciations of Communists," the "mopping up," the "burnings out" . . . at the end of several years of this, there was little left of our village. The people were scattered and could no longer get hold of news about each other. Rumour had it that Sau's wife had gone to Saigon, but then, it was said, she had left again and returned to the Plain of Rushes. It was for this reason that I continued to be the keeper of the comb. I was left looking at this precious object in my hand with a sad heart.

Well, to return to our journey, the engine went chugging on at the stern of the canoe. I would have liked to have another look at the young pilot who held our fate in her hands. The night was neither clear nor really dark. Light clouds floated over the sky allowing the stars to shine through from time to time. In the faint light I looked at the outline of the girl, her delicately rounded face and the eyes which I found strangely disturbing. Peering into these eyes I found the impression growing in me that I was looking at the eyes of someone familiar.

Suddenly there were cries: "Planes! Planes!"

The canoe began to rock. The passengers began fidgeting in alarm.

"Look out!"

"Where are they?"

"There, over the stern. See the light!"

"Attention! Enemy planes!"

The guide slowed the engine, turned round for an instant, then announced, "No, it is only a star in the sky." Her calm voice soothed the general agitation. Her example restored everyone's courage. She had said it so softly, then opened up the throttle.

After the previous journey on foot we were delighted to be able to travel at ease in a canoe, but the thought of aeroplanes always made me nervous. The canoe engine made too much noise. If a plane were to creep up on us out of that sky we wouldn't even hear it.

The canal at this point passed through a part of the plain that had been ruined. No human habitation remained, only occasionally the torn silhouette of a clump of bamboos or some kind of trees. I longed to get through this bit of the journey.

The pilot accelerated the engine, bow waves surged up the prow of the canoe forming on either side long furrows that dragged at the tufts of reeds and beat against the roots and tangled vegetation by the banks.

While everyone was tranquilly enjoying the swift passage through the water the pilot suddenly slowed down and announced "Planes!"

She slid the boat under a tuft of bamboos and stopped the engine. The second canoe, just behind us, followed suit. Now we could distinctly hear the characteristic sound of the Yankee helicopters. It was true, our young pilot had remarkably sharp hearing. It could have been by no means easy to distinguish the still far-off throb of the helicopters through the noise of the outboard motors. The boat plunged and several passengers nearly lost their balance. Our guide reassured us, saying, "They are still some way off, Uncles. Get up the bank and disappear. Find somewhere to hide and while they pass over take care to remain absolutely still." While she was speaking, everyone was jumping to land. I was the last. As I prepared to get out, she said to me, "If you feel inclined you can stay here with me, my Uncle. With only us in the canoe there is nothing to fear."

I don't suppose I would have accepted this invitation from another guide but with her confident bearing I found it more reassuring to remain beside her.

The American helicopters coming from the mouth of the canal, came over gradually. They made more din than a dozen steamers. The glare of their searchlights came nearer and, as is their custom, they came in threes. The front one of the formation to light up the target with its searchlight, while the two others prepared to open fire.

"Pull the leaves right over you and don't move," the girl reminded me. This was the first time I had experienced the full glare of a helicopter's searchlight. When it came, I felt sure that under that dazzling illumination and the shattering throbbing that accompanied it our boat was much too easily visible. I actually saw the bamboo leaves parting with a shudder as though in a blast of air, uncovering a corner of my travelling sack.

"It's all up," I thought as I hunched my shoulders ready to make a plunge for escape. Realising my anxiety the young guide reassured me.

"It's not so easy to see us!"

This time her calm didn't so readily convince me. For an instant I really was about to fling myself into the water, but controlled myself in time. Then the infernal glare faded and the stupifying throbbing grew gradually fainter. The night returned and the mild light of the stars. I remained motionless, fearing the return of the enemy. The girl tried to encourage me.

"They like to pretend to scare the life out of you, but as a matter of fact they see nothing. It is enough to just keep calm and not move."

Then looking out over the marshes, she called in the others. Some of them were soaked. They changed what clothes they could, cursing the Yankees as they did so.

The canoe resumed its journey.

After midnight we continued our journey by land. We went along by the raised paths through rice paddies. The soil in places was very slippery and sometimes we had to wade through mud and water. We kept in close single file, slithering and tumbling in turns. One would just be scrambling to his feet when another took a skid into the rice. We carried our sandals and felt our way step by step.

As we approached a river our guide halted the line and sent two scouts in advance to explore. After about twenty minutes they fell into an ambush. This time the enemy had not remained hidden in the trees by the river, but had taken up positions in the fields. They launched an intense volley of shots. Bullets went whistling over our heads.

"Get down flat!" commanded our guide.

"Comrade Tu, lead the travellers, I shall stay here."

No sooner was the order given than she disappeared. The bullets criss-crossed over our heads in an impenetrable network and passed whizzing over the rice field. We had literally to plant ourselves in the mud. After a moment the shots of a carbine could be heard to the left of us. Instantly the direction of enemy fire altered to that direction and I understood that our guide had gone deliberately to draw the enemy fire.

"Run for it," commanded Tu, the comrade in charge of the party. We ran. I am not accustomed to hand to hand fighting, however at this moment I must say I felt no fear on my own account but could only think about the girl who was our guide.

Our party ran in disorder across the field to get to the line of trees and then to the river. The shooting increased in intensity. I paused to listen intently for the sound of the carbine that the girl was firing. It was not distinguishable from the general din, and I felt my heart begin to beat as though it would burst.

The gunfight was the cause of our arriving in good time at the village. The comrades from D.A. station were arriving at the same time. But we had not long to rest there before moving on.

Our group reformed in an orchard of coconut palms whose ragged leaves had been burned by the Americans with toxic sprays. We were all present. Some had lost their satchels since the river crossing. As for myself I was still all in one piece in spite of my age, and nothing was lost.

We were all tired out and the liaison comrades of the post let us rest until morning. Several didn't even wait to sling their hammocks or even to spread their nets.

For my part I remained in a kind of half sleeping dream. I imagined myself returned to our village. Evidently it was not as I had known it. The neighbours had been chased from their homes and forced to crowd into concentration camps. They had burst free from these disguised prisons to flock back to their homes but could no longer find their gardens and orchards. This much I had heard but had never quite succeeded in bringing it home to my imagination. I remembered the familiar landscape, my last visit there with Sau, the scene of our farewell, the promise he made to the child, the comb which I still kept in my pocket. While these pictures were passing in a dreamlike sequence in my imagination I also turned to wondering about the comrades who had got left behind at the place of the ambush. Particularly, of course, I thought of our young girl leader. She and her comrades . . . . what had happened to them? At last fatigue overcame me and I fell into a deep sleep.

Sometime later the sound of footsteps, voices and laughter startled me awake.

In the sky long clouds were trailing as though the retreating night were dragging slow veils over the rice fields. I was aware of a group of people in animated conversation. I couldn't hear properly what they were saying, but it certainly sounded like an exchange of thrilling stories. Among them I could make out our young guide, her clothes soaked and covered with mud. So here they were, returned from the scene of the battle!

I approached the group as they were about to separate. It was only now that I could at last take a proper look at the girl. She could not have been more than twenty. She came towards me and I at once wanted to tell her of my feelings of affection and admiration for her and also to thank her. I saluted her with a smile and said to her the better to understand her, "Ah, my child, I was so worried about you. Tell me this — whereabouts in the order of your family do you come?"

"I am the eldest, Uncle."

"But then how is it that I heard the comrades calling you also 'youngest sister'?"

"I am at the same time the youngest and the eldest. I am the only one."

"Tell me, what village do you come from? I feel I might have seen you before somewhere."

"I came from the island of Gieng, Uncle."

I started at the name of our village. Looking into her eyes I felt my heart beating strongly and I began to fire questions at her.

"You mean the island of Gieng in the district of Nouveau Manche, in the Long Chan Sa?"

"Yes, Uncle."

"Your name — what is your name?"

"I am called Thu."

"Thu!" I repeated thunderstruck. "Your father is comrade Sau and your mother Madame Binh. Is that so?" The girl stood there amazed to the point of speechlessness. Her large eyes were opened wide, searching my face.

At this moment the comrades from D.A. station called us travellers to resume the journey. I went over to implore them to wait for me a moment, then went back to the girl. We were at this moment both of us still stunned with amazement. She continued to search my face with her large astonished eyes. I could not be wrong, these were unmistakably the eyes of that child.

"How did you know, Uncle?"

I was finding it hard to control my emotion, but I managed to say softly, "I am Uncle Ba . . . . . Do you remember that when your father went away he promised to bring you a comb?"

The girl nodded her head.

"Yes, I remember . . . . . I remember."

In the Resistance it sometimes happens that there are such strange meetings. I looked at her, slowly taking the comb from my pocket.

"Your father sends you this ivory comb. He made it with his own hands."

Her eyes became even rounder as she held out her hands to receive the present. The comb seemed to bring back to her memories of her feelings on that day of separation, for her breathing quickened.

As I watched her holding the comb in her hands, looking at it, my heart contracted with pain. I imagined she must be over-whelmed with unexpected happiness and I wanted to do nothing to blight that happiness. It seemed to me that I must hide the truth.

"Your Daddy continues in good health. He can't come to you, so he sends you this gift."

Young Thu looked at me steadily under her lowered eyelids. She said slowly with trembling lips: "You have made a mistake, I'm afraid, Uncle. This comb did not come from my father."

"Your father is certainly Sau and your mother is called Binh. Isn't that so?"

"Yes." She seemed about to cry, her eyes reddened, but she continued. "If you are not mistaken then you have not told me the truth. I know that my father is dead." She blinked her eyes and tears rolled onto her cheeks.

"I can bear it, Uncle, never fear. I heard about my father's death two years ago. That was when I asked my mother to let me become a liaison agent."

She seemed still to have more to tell me, but her voice failed and she looked at the ground. For my part, utterly confused by the lie I had told, I did not know what more to say and remained silent.

At this moment my travelling companions shouted for me to join them.

Unable to keep them waiting any longer, I had to hurry my adieus. I hastily demanded the address of the young girl, asked for news of her mother and some of her other relatives. We had neither of us recovered from the emotional surprise of this meeting, but at once we had to part again.

Looking into her eyes for the last time I found myself quoting Sau's words. "Come now. Daddy is going away, my child."

I heard no reply from her, but only saw her pale lips move as though to say something.

After marching off for what seemed a long time, I turned my head and saw that she had followed some of the way. She had stopped at the edge of a meadow of young rice. The green blades undulated in gentle waves which seemed to run to her feet to console her.

Behind her, the long ragged fronds of the coconut palms, withered by chemical spray, hung like enormous dry fish bones, while the young palms that had already begun to sprout from the ground looked like a grove of spears.

(Translated by Mary Cowan).

The General Goes Zapping Charlie Cong

Nicholas Tomalin

After a light lunch last Wednesday, General James F. Hollingsworth, of Big Red One, took off in his personal helicopter and killed more Vietnamese than all the troops he commanded.

The story of the General's feat begins in the divisional office, at Ki-Na, twenty miles north of Saigon, where a Medical Corps colonel is telling me that when they collect enemy casualties they find themselves with more than four injured civilians for every wounded Viet Cong — unavoidable in this kind of war.

The General strides in, pins two medals for outstanding gallantry to the chest of one of the colonel's combat doctors. Then he strides off again to his helicopter, and spreads out a polythene-covered map to explain our afternoon's trip.

The General has a big, real American face, reminiscent of every movie general you have seen. He comes from Texas, and is 48. His present rank is Brigadier General, Assistant Division Commander, 1st Infantry Division, United States Army (which is what the big red figure one on his shoulder flash means).

'Our mission today,' says the General, 'is to push those goddam VCs right off Routes 13 and 16. Now you see 13 and 16 running north from Saigon toward the town of Phuoc Vinh, where we keep our artillery. When we got here first we prettied up those roads, and cleared Charlie Cong right out so we could run supplies up.

'I guess we've been hither and thither with all our operations since, an' the ol' VC he's reckoned he could creep back. He's been puttin' out propaganda he's goin' to interdict our right of passage along those routes. So this day we aim to zapp him, and zapp him, and zapp him again till we've zapped him right back where he came from. Yes, sir. Let's go.'

The General's UH 18 helicopter carries two pilots, two 60-calibre machine-gunners, and his aide, Dennis Gillman, an apple-cheeked subaltern from California. It also carries the General's own M 16 carbine (hanging on a strut), two dozen smoke-bombs, and a couple of CS anti-personnel gas-bombs, each as big as a small dustbin. Just beside the General is a radio console where he can tune in on orders issued by battalion commanders flying helicopters just beneath him, and company commanders in helicopters just below them.

Under this interlacing of helicopters lies the apparently peaceful landscape beside Routes 13 and 16, filled with farmhouses and peasants hoeing rice and paddy fields.

So far today, things haven't gone too well. Companies Alpha, Bravo and Charlie have assaulted a suspected Viet Cong HQ, found a few tunnels but no enemy.

The General sits at the helicopter's open door, knees apart, his shiny black toecaps jutting out into space, rolls a filtertip cigarette to-and-fro in his teeth, and thinks.

'Put me down at Battalion HQ,' he calls to the pilot.

'There's sniper fire reported on choppers in that area, General.'

'Goddam the snipers, just put me down.'

Battalion HQ at the moment is a defoliated area of four acres packed with tents, personnel carriers, helicopters and milling GIs. We settle into the smell of crushed grass. The General leaps out and strides through his troops.

'Why General, excuse me, we didn't expect you here,' says a sweating major.

'You killed any 'Cong yet?'

'Well no General, I guess he's just too scared of us today. Down the road a piece we've hit trouble, a bulldozer's fallen through a bridge, and trucks coming through a village knocked the canopy off a Buddhist pagoda. Saigon radioed us to repair that temple before proceeding — in the way of civic action, General. That put us back an hour . . .'

'Yeah. Well Major, you spread out your perimeter here a bit, then get to killin' VC's will you?'

Back through the crushed grass to the helicopter.

'I don't know how you think about war. The way I see it, I'm just like any other company boss, gingering up the boys all the time, except I don't make money. I just kill people, and save lives.'

In the air the General chews two more filtertips and looks increasingly forlorn. No action on Route 16, and another Big Red One general has got his helicopter in to inspect the collapsed bridge before ours.

'Swing us back along again,' says the General.

'Reports of fire on choppers ahead, sir. Smoke flare near spot. Strike coming in.'

'Go find that smoke.'

A plume of white rises in the midst of dense tropical forest, with a Bird Dog spotter plane in attendance. Route 16 is to the right; beyond it a large settlement of red-tiled houses.

'Strike coming in, sir.'

Two F105 jets appear over the horizon in formation, split,

then one passes over the smoke, dropping a trail of silver, fish-shaped canisters. After four seconds' silence, light orange fire explodes in patches along an area of fifty yards wide by three-quarters of a mile long. Napalm.

The trees and bushes burn, pouring dark oily smoke into the sky. The second plane dives and fire covers the entire strip of dense forest.

'Aaaaah,' cries the General. 'Nice. Nice. Very neat. Come in low, let's see who's left down there.'

'How do you know for sure the Viet Cong snipers were in that strip you burned?'

'We don't. The smoke position was a guess. That's why we zapp the whole forest.'

'But what if there was someone, a civilian, walking through there?'

'Aw come son, you think there's folks just sniffing flowers in tropical vegetation like that? With a big operation on here-abouts? Anyone left down there, he's Charlie Cong all right.'

I point at a paddy field full of peasants less than a mile away.

'That's different son. We know they're genuine.'

The pilot shouts: 'General, half right, two running for that bush.'

'I see them. Down, down, goddam you.'

In one movement he yanks his M 16 off the hanger, slams in a clip of cartridges and leans right out of the door, hanging on his seatbelt to fire one long burst in the general direction of the bush.

'General, there's a hole, maybe a bunker, down there.'

'Smokebomb, circle, shift it.'

'But General, how do you know those aren't just frightened peasants?'

'Running? Like that? Don't give me a pain. The clips, the clips, where in hell are the cartridges in this ship?'

The aide drops a smoke canister, the General finds his ammunition and the starboard machine-gunner fires rapid bursts into the bush, his tracers bouncing up off the ground round it.

We turn clockwise in ever tighter, lower circles, everyone firing. A shower of spent cartridge cases leaps from the General's carbine to drop, lukewarm, on my arm.

'I . . . WANT . . . YOU . . . TO . . . SHOOT . . . RIGHT . . . UP . . . THE . . . ASS . . . OF . . . THAT . . . HOLE . . . GUNNER.'

Fourth time round the tracers flow right inside the tiny sandbagged opening, tearing the bags, filling it with sand and smoke.

The General falls back off his seatbelt into his chair, suddenly relaxed, and lets out an oddly feminine, gentle laugh. 'That's it,' he says, and turns to me, squeezing his thumb and finger into the

18

sign of a French chef's ecstasy.

We circle now above a single-storey building made of dried reeds. The first burst of fire tears the roof open, shatters one wall into fragments of scattered straw, and blasts the farmyard full of chickens into dismembered feathers.

'Zapp, zapp, zapp,' cries the General. He is now using semi-automatic fire, the carbine bucking in his hands.

Pow, pow, pow, sounds the gun. All the noises of this war have an unaccountably Texan ring.

'Gas bomb.'

Lieutenant Gillman leans his canister out of the door. As the pilot calls, he drops it. An explosion of white vapour spreads across the wood a full hundred yards downwind.

'Jesus wept, lootenant, that's no good.'

Lieutenant Gillman immediately clambers across me to get the second gas bomb, pushing me sideways into his own port-side seat. In considerable panic I fumble with an unfamiliar seatbelt as the helicopter banks round at an angle of fifty degrees. The second gas bomb explodes perfectly, beside the house, covering it with vapour.

'There's nothing alive in there,' says the General. 'Or they'd be skedaddling. Yes there is, by golly.'

For the first time I see the running figure, bobbing and sprinting across the farmyard towards a clump of trees dressed in black pyjamas. No hat. No shoes.

'Now hit the tree.'

We circle five times. Branches drop off the tree, leaves fly, its trunk is enveloped with dust and tracer flares. Gillman and the General are now firing carbines side by side in the doorway. Gillman offers me his gun: No thanks.

Then a man runs from the tree, in each hand a bright red flag which he waves desperately above his head.

'Stop, stop, he's quit,' shouts the General, knocking the machine-gun so traces erupt into the sky.

'I'm going down to take him. Now watch it everyone, keep firing roundabout, this may be an ambush.'

We sink swiftly into the field beside the tree, each gunner firing cautionary bursts into the bushes. The figure walks towards us.

'That's a Cong for sure,' cries the General in triumph and with one deft movement grabs the man's short black hair and yanks him off his feet, inboard. The prisoner falls across Lieutenant Gillman and into the seat beside me.

The red flags I spotted from the air are his hands, bathed solidly in blood. Further blood is pouring from under his shirt, over his trousers.

Now we are safely in the air again. Our captive cannot be more than sixteen years old, his head just about comes up to the white name patch — Hollingsworth — on the General's chest. He is dazed, in shock. His eyes calmly look first at the General, then at the Lieutenant, then at me. He resembles a tiny, fine-boned wild animal. I have to keep my hand firmly pressed against his shoulder to hold him upright. He is quivering. Sometimes his left foot, from some nervous impulse, bangs hard against the helicopter wall. The Lieutenant applies a tourniquet to his right arm.

'Radio base for an ambulance. Get the information officer with a camera. I want this Commie bastard alive till we get back . . . just stay with us till we talk to you, baby.'

The General pokes with his carbine first at the prisoner's cheek to keep his head upright, then at the base of his shirt.

'Look at that now,' he says, turning to me. 'You still thinking about innocent peasants? Look at the weaponry.'

Around the prisoner's waist is a webbing belt, with four clips of ammunition, a water bottle (without stopper), a tiny roll of bandages, and a propaganda leaflet which later turns out to be a set of Viet Cong songs, with a twenty piastre note (about 1s. 6d.) folded in it.

Lieutenant Gillman looks concerned. 'It's OK, you're OK,' he mouths at the prisoner, who at that moment turns to me and with a surprisingly vigorous gesture waves his arm at my seat. He wants to lie down.

By the time I have fastened myself into yet another seat we are back at the landing pad. Ambulance orderlies come aboard, administer morphine, and rip open his shirt. Obviously a burst of fire has shattered his right arm up at the shoulder. The cut shirt now allows a large bulge of blue-red tissue to fall forward, its surface streaked with white nerve fibres and chips of bone (how did he ever manage to wave that arm in surrender?).

When the ambulance has driven off the General gets us all posed round the nose of the chopper for a group photograph like a gang of successful fishermen, then clambers up into the cabin again, at my request, for a picture to show just how he zapped those VCs. He is euphoric.

'Jeez I'm so glad you was along, that worked out just dandy. I've been written up time and time again back in the States for shootin' up VCs, but no one's been along with me like you before.'

We even find a bullet hole in one of the helicopter rotor blades. 'That's proof positive they was firin' at us all the time. An' firin' on us first, boy. So much for your fellers smellin' flowers.'

He gives me the Viet Cong's water bottle as souvenir and

proof. 'That's a chicom bottle, that one. All the way from Peking.'

Later that evening the General calls me to his office to tell me the prisoner had to have his arm amputated, and is now in the hands of the Vietnamese authorities, as regulations dictate. Before he went under, he told the General's interpreters that he was part of a hardcore regular VC company whose mission was to mine Route 16, cut it up, and fire at helicopters.

The General is magnanimous in his victory over my squeamish civilian worries.

'You see son, I saw rifles on that first pair of running men. Didn't tell you that at the time. And, by the way you mustn't imagine there could have been ordinary farm folk in that house, when you're as old a veteran as I am you get to know about those things by instinct. I agree there was chickens for food with them, strung up on a pole. You didn't see anything bigger, like a pig or a cow did yuh? Well then.'

The General wasn't certain whether further troops would go to the farmhouse that night to check who died, although patrols would be near there.

It wasn't safe moving along Route 16 at night, there was another big operation elsewhere the next day. Big Red One is always on the move.

'But when them VC come back harassin' that Route 16 why, we'll zapp them again. And when they come back after that we'll zapp them again.'

'Wouldn't it be easier just to stay there all the time?'

'Why, son, we haven't enough troops as it is.'

'The Koreans manage it.'

'Yeah, but they've got a smaller area to protect. Why Big Red One ranges right over — I mean up to the Cambodian Border. There ain't no place on that map we ain't been.

'I'll say perhaps your English generals wouldn't think my way of war is all that conventional, would they? Well, this is a new kind of war, flexible, quickmoving. Us generals must be on the spot to direct our troops. The helicopter adds a new dimension to battle.

'There's no better way to fight than goin' out to shoot VCs. An' there's nothing I love better than killin' 'Cong. No, sir.'

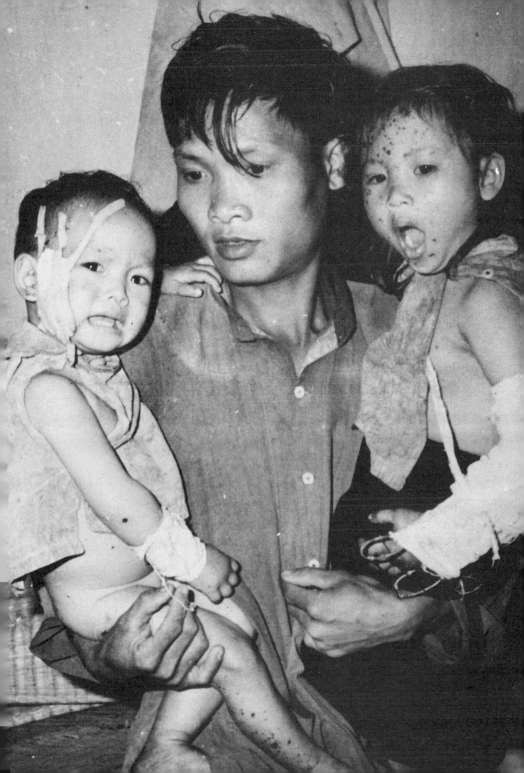

Peppermints and Daisy Chains

Adrian Mitchell

Thinks: I'll Finish These Viets By Building an Electronically Operated Physical Barrier Right Along Their Seventeenth Parallel!!!

1. Thousands of miles of invisible fencing
   Distinguishable only by the balding badness of the earth
   And a slight electric shimmer in the air.

   But if you throw raw hamburger towards the sky
   It comes down grilled.

2. The marine shouted:
   'I don't mind fighting Charlie,
   But not with my back to a goddam
   Electronically operated physical barrier.'

3. We have stopped lifting our electronic barrier
   For one hour daily at Checkpoint Harold.
   We don't mind the refugee double-deckers heading north,
   But sod this constant rumbling southwards
   Of enormous invisible wooden horses.

4. If the barrier fails
   We are going to bring in volcanoes.

5. 'I just pissed against that
   Electronically operated physical barrier,'
   Boasted the police dog to his bitch,
   'And eighty-two square miles got devastated.'

6. Tom Sawyer drew a line in the dust with his toe:
   'Step over that and I'll burn your skin off.'

7. What we really need
   Is an electronically operated physical barrier
   Around the United States.

To Whom It May Concern

I was run over by the truth one day.
Ever since the accident I've walked this way
    So stick my legs in plaster
    Tell me lies about Vietnam.

Heard the alarm clock screaming with pain,
Couldn't find myself so I went back to sleep again
    So fill my ears with silver
    Stick my legs in plaster
    Tell me lies about Vietnam.

Every time I shut my eyes all I see is flames.
Made a marble phone book and I carved all the names
    So coat my eyes with butter
    Fill my ears with silver
    Stick my legs in plaster
    Tell me lies about Vietnam.

I smell something burning, hope it's just my brains.
They're only dropping peppermints and daisy-chains
    So stuff my nose with garlic
    Coat my eyes with butter
    Fill my ears with silver
    Stick my legs in plaster
    Tell me lies about Vietnam.

Where were you at the time of the crime?
Down by the Cenotaph drinking slime
    So chain my tongue with whisky
    Stuff my nose with garlic
    Coat my eyes with butter
    Fill my ears with silver
    Stick my legs in plaster
    Tell me lies about Vietnam.

You put your bombers in, you put your conscience out,
You take the human being and you twist it all about
    So scrub my skin with women
    Chain my tongue with whisky
    Stuff my nose with garlic
    Coat my eyes with butter
    Fill my ears with silver
    Stick my legs in plaster
    Tell me lies about Vietnam.

Zapping the Cong

I'm really rockin' the Delta
From coast to coast.
Got em crawling for shelter,
Got em burning like toast.
And the President told me
It wouldn't take long,
But I know I'm in heaven
When I'm Zapping the Cong.

Zapping the Cong
Back where they belong.
Hidé your yellow asses
When you hear my song.
All over the jungle,
Up to old Haiphong,
Been crapping jelly petrol,
I been zap-zap-zap-zap Zapping the Cong.

Had a bomb in my 'copter
Called Linda B.
Saw a village and dropped her
On a mess of VC.
But I always say sorry
When I get it wrong.
Then I got to be zooming,
'Cause I'm Zapping the Cong.

Zapping the Cong
Back where they belong.
Hide your yellow asses
When you hear my song.
All over the jungle,
Up to old Haiphong,
Been crapping jelly petrol,
I been zap-zap-zap-zap Zapping the Cong.

I had a dream about going
With Ho Chi Minh.
But I'll only be crowing
When I'm zapping Pekin.
I'll be spreading my jelly
With a happy song
'Cause I'm screwing all Asia
When I'm Zapping the Cong.

Zapping the Cong
Back where they belong.
Hide your yellow asses
When you hear my song.
All over the jungle,
Up to old Haiphong,
Been crapping jelly petrol,
I been zap-zap-zap-zap Zapping the Cong.

Make and Break

Pass me the stethoscope of Albert Schweitzer,
Pass me the armoury of Mickey Spillane.
Put the mothers through the bacon-slicer
Pick up the pieces and fit them together again.

Want to be humane, but we're only human.
Off with the old skin, on with the new.
We maim by night.
We heal by day.
Just the same as you.

Fill all the area with whirling metal,
Five thousand razor-blades are slashing like rain.
Mr Hyde has a buddy called Jekyll
Picks up the pieces and fits them together again.

Want to be humane, but we're only human.
Off with the old skin, on with the new.
We maim by night.
We heal by day.
Just the same as you.

We treat the enemy like real blood brothers
God made the family a blessing and pain.
Wives and husbands vivisect each other,
Pick up the pieces and fit them together again.

Want to be humane, but we're only human.
Off with the old skin, on with the new.
We maim by night.
We heal by day.
Just the same as you.

Cease-Fire

The outside of my body was half-eaten
by the fire which clings as tight as skin.
The fire has turned some of my skin
into black scab bits of roughness
and some pale bits, smooth as plastic,
which no one dares touch
except me and the doctor.

Everyone who looks at me is scared.
That's not because I want to hurt people
but because so much of me
looks like the meat of a monster.

I was walking to the market.
Then I was screaming.
They found me screaming.
They put out the flames on my skin.
They laid me on a stretcher and I cried:
Not on my back!

So they turned me over and I cried:
Not on my front!

A doctor put a needle in my arm
and my mind melted
and I fell into a furnace of dreams of furnaces.

When I woke up I was in a white hospital.
Everything I wanted to say scared me
and I did not want to scare the others
in that white hospital,
so I said nothing. I cried as quietly as I could.

Months passed over my head
and bombers passed over my head
and people came and said they were my parents
and they found out the right places on my face
where I could bear to be kissed.

And I pretended I could see them
but I couldn't really look out of my eyes
but only inwards, inwards into my head
where the flames still clung and hurt.

And the voice of the flames said:
You are meat.
You are ugly meat.
Your body cannot grow into loveliness.
Nobody could love such ugly meat.
Only ugly meat could love such ugly meat.
Better be stewed for soup and eaten.

And months passed over my head
and the bombers passed over my head
and the voices of the flames began to flicker
and I began to believe
the people who said they were my parents
were my parents.
And one day I threw myself forward
so that I sat up in bed, for the first time,
and hurled my arms around my mother,
and however the skin of my chest howled out its pain
I held her, I held her, I held her
and knew she was my mother.
And I forgot that I was monster meat
and I knew she did not know that I was monster meat.

I held her, I held her.
And, sweet sun which blesses all the world -
all the flames faded.
The flames of my skin
and the flames inside my head -
all the flames faded
and I was flooded
with love for my mother
who did not know
that I was monster meat.

And so, in the love-flood, I let go of my mother
and fell back upon my pillow
and I rolled my head to the left side

and saw a child, or it might have been an old man,
eating his rice with his only arm
and I rolled my head to the right side
and saw another child, or she might have been an old woman,
who had no eyes,
being fed through the arm from a tube from a red bottle -
and I loved them, and, flooded with love
I started to sing
the song of the game I used to play with my friends
in the long-ago days before the flames came:

One, one, I bounce the ball.
Once for the cobbler at the corner.
Two, two, I bounce the ball.
Twice for the fisherman on the river.
Three, three, I bounce the ball.
Three times for my golden lover -

And had to stop singing.
Throat choked with vomit.

And then the flames exploded again all over my skin
and then the flames exploded again inside my head
and I burned, sweet sun, sweet mother, I burned.

Sweet sun, which blesses all the world,
this was one of the people of Vietnam.
Make him or her whatever game you like -
he or she is dead.

The one-armed man or boy survives.
The blind woman or girl
whose body needs a change of blood each day
survives.

I suppose we love each other.
We're stupid if we don't.
We have a choice -
Either to choke to death on our own vomit
or to become one
with the sweet sun, which blesses all the world.

The Real War Is Between Those Who Catch Hell and Those Who Dish It Out

David Harris and Ron Kovic

A lieutenant took Ron Kovic's detail out to search for sappers across the river. There was a village on the far bank and the colonel was worried someone would dive in and put a mine to the marine boats. A hundred meters from the village, the patrol saw the light of a small fire. It was inside a hootch and it wasn't supposed to be there. The village had been ordered to keep lights out. The platoon spread out along a paddy dike and watched. Word was passed to hold fire and the lieutenant set off an illumination flare. Just as the flare lit, someone to Ron's left fucked up and let go. That shot set the whole line on fire for 30 seconds at full automatic. When they finished, Ron and Leroy were sent up to check the hootch.

Inside the broken bamboo, there was an old man with the top of his head shot away. Two kids were on either side of him. One's foot just dangled. The other had taken a round in the stomach that came out his ass. The hootch's floor was covered with blood.

When the platoon crossed the paddy and saw it, the marines melted into lumps. Some dropped their weapons and only Leroy talked. "Jesus Christ," he whined. "What'd we do. We've killed an old man and some kids."

The lieutenant yelled to form up in a 360 but Leroy kept moaning and no one else moved. The villagers started to come out of their huts and scream at the marines. It took the lieutenant five minutes to round the patrol into shape. After they called a chopper for the kid who was still breathing, the platoon went inside the wire. Sgt. Kovic laid in his bunker all night and wanted to give it up. He wanted the referee to blow the whistle and call time out until he'd had a chance to think it over.

But wars don't work that way. Ron reported to the colonel in the morning and asked to be taken off patrols. The colonel said no. Instead the platoon got a week in camp and Sgt. Kovic was ordered to get his shit together and act like a marine.

The platoon didn't go back to action until January 20th. When they did, it was in the afternoon. January 20th started late but turned into a big day, about as big a day as there will ever be in the life of Sgt. Ron Kovic. It was a day that made all the ones after it very different from the ones that went before.

Word was that the NVA had the South Vietnamese Popular Forces pinned down by the village. Ron volunteered his men to take the point and lead the company's sweep. Another company was moving north from the river bank through the village grave-yard. The platoon spread out and headed towards the treeline 100 metres off. Ron was on the right with just one man further over than himself. Everyone was out in the open when January 20th exploded. Ron couldn't forget it now if he wanted to.

"The people on the amtracs got hit first" is the way he remembers it. "I heard the pop . . . pop . . . pop as the mortars left their tubes and the crashing as they hit around the tracks. Then rounds started cracking around us. I couldn't tell if they were coming from the village or the treeline, so I fired both places. I was completely out in the open.

"All we could do was take ground and return fire. After a little bit, I heard a loud crack right next to me and my whole leg went numb. A .30 caliber bullet had gone in the front of my foot and come out the heel. It took a piece out the size of a silver dollar. My foot was all smashed. I stayed standing as long as I could but then it began to feel like it was on fire. I went to a prone position and kept using my rifle until it jammed from the sand.

"When I couldn't get a round into the chamber, I decided to stand and see where the rest of my platoon was. I slammed the rifle down and pushed myself up with it. Just as I got my arms straight, I heard a huge crack next to my ear. It was like getting hit with an express train. My whole body started vibrating. Another .30 caliber bullet had hit my right shoulder, passed through my lung and severed my spinal cord into two pieces. My whole body seemed to have left me. I felt like I was somewhere up in the air.

"I closed my eyes for just a second, then I started to breathe. My lung was collapsed so I just took little breaths. Slow little sucks. All I could think was that I didn't want to die. I couldn't think of nothin' else. I waited to die. I mean I just waited for it all to black out, for all the things that are supposed to happen when you die. I couldn't believe what was going on. Where was my body? I must've been hit with a mortar. That was it, a mortar. It had ground up everything below my chest.

"Then I moved my hands behind me and I felt legs. I felt legs but they didn't feel back. They were my legs. There was something wrong but I couldn't explain it. My body was there but I couldn't feel it. Then I got real excited. It was still there. I wasn't going to bleed to death. My body was still there.

"The next thing I knew, Leroy was over me. He was bandaging my shoulder.

"'I can't feel my body,' I said.

"'It's all right, Sarge,' he said. 'You're gonna be all right. Pretty soon you'll be back in the States with all the broads.'

"When he got the bandage on, he split towards the treeline with rounds cracking all around him.

"After Leroy, I heard Palmer calling me from off to my left. 'Hey Sarge,' he said. 'We've got to get the hell out of here.'

"'I can't move my legs,' I screamed.

"'Come on, Sarge,' Palmer kept yelling. 'Let's go. Let's get outta here.'

"'I can't feel my body,' I said. Then I heard a crack and Palmer screamed.

"'Are you hit?' I yelled.

"Palmer yelled back. 'They shot my finger off. They shot my goddamn finger off.' After that I guess he left. I didn't hear him no more.

"I lay there for what seemed like hours. Once, somebody ran up in back of me. 'Hey,' he said. 'Hey Sarge, you all right?' Then I heard another crack and he seemed to fall on the back of me. I couldn't feel it but I heard. Someone from my left yelled, 'He's dead, Sarge. They shot him through the heart.' He was a marine from the company who'd run all the way up. I yelled for everybody to stop coming. I don't know if they heard, but I yelled. I was being used as bait. Other than that, I felt nothing. I just wanted to live. I tried to calm myself. I felt cheated. I felt cheated to die. Twenty fucking years old and they were taking my life away from me.

"Then a black man came running up. He grabbed me and threw me over his shoulder. He started dragging me back. He was a big black man. Big black arms. Big black hands. All I can remember is staring up at the sky and the sky sort of spinning and jumping. I could just feel the top of my body. I felt the sun in my face and him picking me up and throwing me down. All the time he was yelling, 'You motherfuckers. Fuckers. Fuckers. Goddamn motherfuckers.' And me screaming the same thing. 'Motherfuckers. Motherfuckers.'

"Finally he threw me one last time in a hole and a corpsman jumped in on my chest. He'd been running all over and he was out of his head. I told him I felt I'd made it so far and that was the roughest part. I told him I was gonna live."

By the next morning, Sgt. Kovic had been given the last rites of the Catholic Church and gone on the operating table. He was in the intensive care ward at Marble Mountain in Da Nang. He'd been brought there by choppers with tubes in his lungs and IVs all over his body. There was a Korean (who'd hit a booby trap) in the bed to his left. When he wasn't babbling in sing-song, the Korean waved his two remaining fingers over his head until he died. Then a black pilot took the Korean's place.

Ron watched the pilot die too. The corpsmen surrounded the bed and one began to beat on the pilot's chest with his fists. They brought a machine over and attached it to his heart but it didn't seem to do much better. The corpsman went back to his hands and pounded as hard as he knew how. After a half-hour, the medic gave up. Ron could see his white jacket and hear him laughing like the Bob Hope show. The corpsman had to laugh. He pounded on chests all day long. The last Ron saw of the black pilot was the sheet they covered him with and the sound of the body cart, squeaking across the linoleum.

After that, Ron was sure he'd die if he stayed at Marble Mountain. Living meant doing everything right, so Sgt. Kovic listed his do's and dont's on a Red Cross pad. The nurse turned him over every four hours and Ron never complained. He was going to be the perfect patient who recovers miraculously. The morphine helped. He got his syringe every 120 minutes. When he was waiting for his shot, Ron Kovic noticed that he couldn't feel his dick anymore. All day long, he explored his floppy body and checked to see if it had come back while he was asleep. It never did.

When the doctors asked Ron how he felt he said he felt great. Good enough to leave intensive care anyway. In desperation, Sgt. Kovic finally stuck his thermometer in an ice bucket and the reading was low enough to go to Japan. With Da Nang behind him, Ron knew he was going to live. He didn't know how that living was going to be, but right then he didn't care.

Before the plane left Marble Mountain, a general came down the ward, distributing Purple Hearts, bed by bed. The general's shoes were shined and he had a private with him. The private carried a polaroid camera and took pictures the men could send home to their families. The general handed Ron a medal, the private took a picture and Ron put the ribbon under his pillow.

Then the general went to the bed next door. There was a 19-year-old marine in it. He'd had the top of his skull blown loose. The 19-year-old's brain was wrapped in wet towels. He babbled like a two-year-old and pissed in his sheets. Ron waited to see if the general's private would leave a picture.

He did. The private told the nurse to send it on to the marine's mom and dad.

Back in the States a year and a half later, Ron moved to

Los Angeles and called the office of Vietnam Veterans Against the War. While he dialed, he thought about a guy named Willie.

Willie was just a head. To listen to Willie you had to put a cork in his throat and your ears next to his lips. As Ron was leaving hospital, Willie stopped him at his bed. Ron put the cork in and listened.

"Don't let them do it to anybody else," Willie said.

When the phone answered, Ron said he wanted to join and do anything he could to stop the war.

Ron meant it. He manned tables and spoke at high schools. He told them how he'd been the Massapequa flash and the push-up body. He told them how he'd sung about the "Halls of Montezuma" and the "Shores of Tripoli" and how it was a lie. He told whoever would listen and half those who wouldn't.

Ron felt better than he'd felt in a long time. He liked the folks, like he was one of them. He didn't feel like a freak and he wondered why it had taken so long for him to find out. His new life gave Ron a chance to meet his country again. One such meeting on Wilshire Boulevard drove the last of the bald eagle from Ron Kovic's mind. It happened in front of the headquarters for Richard Nixon's re-election.

The picket started at 11 a.m. and by noon there was quite a crowd and almost as many cops. And these weren't any run-of-the-mill-bust-a-drunk-on-a-street-corner cops. It was the L.A.P.D. and anybody west of Barstow knows the L.A.P.D. doesn't take no for an answer.

The ones Ron met were young, undercover, and tried special hard. They moved in the crowd and took notes. Ron was up the block with a line of people who had wheeled over the cross street and blocked traffic. The blue line of police moved their way and they scattered back to the sidewalk. As soon as the cops leaned to the cross street, the people on Wilshire did the same thing and the police scurried back. It didn't take long for the L.A.P.D. to tire of the game. The captain gave an order to disperse and the people decided to take it. The blue men had their clubs out and their goggles on: two very bad signs. The decision was made to go to McArthur Park. Ron wheeled the word up to the cops.

"We're leaving," he said. "We're going to obey the order to disperse."

With that, the line of signs made its own slow way back down the boulevard. Ron stayed at the back, making sure everybody got out all right. It was then that he met the L.A.P.D. up so close there was no way to mistake what he saw. The two longhaired ones came up from his back. The first grabbed Ron's chair. The second said, "You're under arrest," and started banging the handcuffs on Ron's wrists.

"What are you doing?" Ron said. "We're leaving."

The back of the crowd saw what was happening and ran to help. That set off a whistle and the blue line charged into a big circle with Ron inside. He was dumped out of his chair and onto the street. All Ron could think to do was shout.

"I'm a Vietnam veteran," he yelled. "I fought in the DMZ. I'm paralyzed. Don't you know what you're doing?"

The L.A.P.D. didn't shout back. The red-haired one pulled Ron's hands behind his back and locked them. Then the blue circle made a wedge and headed across the street with Ron in tow. A cop had each shoulder and Ron's head bobbed up and down off the asphalt. The people who tried to help said they saw the police beat Ron's body with their sticks, but Ron didn't feel it. He felt the curb when his forehead hit it and then all of a sudden he felt lifted up and into a squad car. They propped him up in the front seat. He immediately flopped over into the dashboard and panted.

"I have no stomach muscles," he said. "With my hands in back of me, I can't sit up. I can't hardly breathe either." Ron had to talk in a grunt.

The cop shoved him up straight. "Sit up," he said.

Ron flopped back over. "I'm a veteran," he wheezed. "Don't you see what you're doing to me? I'm paralyzed."

"Sit up," the cop said and rammed Ron against the Ford's seat. Ron flopped back. "I said sit up you commie son of a bitch." The L.A.P.D. bounced Ron back and forth all the way to the station. At the booking desk, the cop asked the turnkey where to put the crippled one.

"Take him up on the roof and throw him off," the turnkey said.

They didn't. But it wasn't because they didn't want to. When Ron left five days later, the turnkey looked at him from behind his jowels.

"They shoulda let you die over there," he said. "You shoulda died and never come back."

The Teeth Mother
Naked At Last

Robert Bly

I

Massive engines lift beautifully from the deck.
Wings appear over the trees, wings with eight hundred rivets.

Engines burning a thousand gallons of gasoline a minute sweep
    over the huts with dirt floors.

The chickens feel the new fear deep in the pits of their beaks.
Buddha with Padma Sambhava.
Slate ships float on the China Sea,
gray bodies born in Roanoke,
    the ocean to both sides expanding,
    "buoyed on the dense marine."

Helicopters flutter overhead. The death-
bee is coming. Super Sabres
like knots of neurotic energy sweep
around and return.
This is Hamilton's triumph.
This is the advantage of a centralised bank.

B-52's come from Guam. All the teachers
die in flames. The hopes of Tolstoy fall asleep in the ant-heap.
Do not ask for mercy.

Now the time comes to look into the past-tunnels,
the hours given and taken in school,
the scuffles in coatrooms,
foam leaps from his nostrils,
 now we come to the scum you take from the mouths of the dead,

now we sit beside the dying, and hold their hands, there is hardly
    time for goodbye,
the staff sergeant from North Carolina is dying—you hold his
    hand,
he knows the mansions of the dead are empty, he has an empty
    place inside him, created one night when his parents came home

drunk, he uses half his skin to cover it,
as you try to protect a balloon from sharp objects . . .
Artillery shells explode. Napalm canisters roll end over end.
800 steel pellets fly through the vegetable walls.
The six-hour infant puts his fists instinctively to his eyes to keep
    out the light.
But the room explodes,
the children explode.
Blood leaps on the vegetable walls.

Yes, I know, blood leaps on the walls—
No need to cry at that—
Do you cry at the wind pouring out of Canada?
Do you cry at the reeds shaken at the edges of the sloughs?
The marine battalion enters.
This happens when the seasons change,
 this happens when the leaves begin to drop from the trees
    too early
"Kill them: I don't want to see anything moving."
That happens when the ice begins to show its teeth in the ponds
that happens when the heavy layers of lake water press down on
    the fish's head, and send him deeper, where his tail swirls
    slowly, and his brain passes him pictures of heavy reeds, of
    vegetation fallen on vegetation . . . .

Hamilton saw all this in detail:
"Every banana tree slashed, every cooking utensil smashed, every
    mattress cut."

Now the Marine knives sweep around like sharp-edged jets;
   how easily they slash open the rice bags,
the mattresses . . . .
ducks are killed with $150 shotguns.
Old women watch the soldiers.

II

Excellent Roman knives slip along the ribs,
A stronger man starts to jerk up the strips of flesh.
Let's hear it again, you believe in the Father, the Son, and the
    Holy Ghost?
A long scream unrolls.
More.
From the political point of view, democratic institutions are being
    built in Vietnam, wouldn't you agree?

A green parrot shudders under the fingernails.
Blood jumps in the pocket.
The scream lashes like a tail.

"Let us not be deterred from our task by the voices of dissent . . ."
The whines of jets
pierce like a long needle.
As soon as the President finishes his press conference, black
    wings carry off the words,
bits of flesh still clinging to them.

The ministers lie, the professors lie, the television lies,
    the priests lie . . . .
These lies mean that the country wants to die.
Lie after lie starts out into the prairie grass,
like enormous trains of Conestoga wagons . . . .

And a long desire for death flows out, guiding
the enormous caravans from beneath,
stringing together the vague and foolish words.

It is a desire to eat death,
to gobble it down,
to rush on it like a cobra with mouth open,

It's a desire to take death inside,
to feel it burning inside, pushing out velvety hairs.
like a clothes brush in the intestines.

This is the thrill that leads the President on to lie.

The Chief Executive enters: the Press Conference begins:
First the President lies about the date the Appalachian Mountains
    rose.
Then he lies about the population of Chicago, then about the
    weight of the adult eagle, next about the acreage of the
    Everglades,

He lies about the number of fish taken every year in the Arctic,
    he has private information about which city is the capital
    of Wyoming, he lies about the birthplace of Attila the Hun,

He lies about the composition of the amniotic fluid, he insists
    that Luther was never a German, and insists that only the
    Protestants sold indulgences,

That Pope Leo X *wanted* to reform the church, but the
  "liberal elements" prevented him,

That the Peasants' War was fomented by Italians from the North.
And the Attorney General lies about the time the sun sets.

This is only the deep longing for death.
It is the longing for someone to come and take us by the hand
  to where they all are sleeping:
where the Egyptian Pharaohs are asleep, and your own mother,
and all those disappeared children, who used to go around with
  you in a swing at grade school . . . .

Do not be angry at the President—he is longing to take in his
  hand the locks of death hair—
to meet his own children sleeping, or unborn . . . .
He is drifting sideways towards the dusty places.

III

That's what it's like for a rich country to make war,
That's what it's like to bomb huts (afterwards described as
  "structures")
That's what it's like to kill marginal farmers (afterwards described
  as "Communists")

This is what it's like to watch the altimeter needle going mad

*Baron 25, this is 81. Are there any friendlies in the area? 81 from
25, negative on the friendlies. I'd like you to take out as many
structures as possible located in those trees within 200 meters
east and west of my smoke mark.*

Diving, the green earth swinging, cheeks hanging back, red pins
  blossoming ahead of us, 20 millimeter cannon fire, leveling off,
  rice fields shooting by like telephone poles, smoke rising,
  hut roofs loom up huge as landing fields, slugs going in, half the
  huts on fire, figures running, palm trees burning, shooting past,
  up again; blue sky, cloud mountains

That is what it's like to have a gross national product

It's because a hospital room in the average American city now
  costs $60 a day that we bombed hospitals in the North

It's because the aluminium window-shade business is doing so
   well in the United States that we roll fire over entire villages

It's because the milk trains coming in to New Jersey hit the right
   switches every day that the best Vietnamese men are cut in
   two by American bullets that follow each other like freight cars

This is what it's like to send firebombs down in 110° heat from
   air-conditioned cockpits,

This is what it's like to be told to fire into a reed hut with an
   automatic weapon,

It's because we have new packaging for smoked oysters that
   bomb holes appear in the rice paddies

It is because we have so few women sobbing in back rooms,
because we have so few children's heads torn apart by
   high-velocity bullets,
because we have so few tears falling on our own hands
that the Super Sabre turns and screams down toward the earth

It's because tax-payers move to the suburbs that we transfer
   populations
The Marines use cigarette lighters to light the thatched roofs
   of huts because so many Americans own their own homes.

IV

I see a car rolling toward a rock wall.
The treads in the face begin to crack.
We all feel like tyres being run down roads under heavy cars.

The teenager imagines herself floating through the
   Seven Spheres.
Oven doors are found
open.
Soot collects over the doorframe, has children, takes courses,
goes mad, and dies.
There is a black silo inside our bodies, revolving fast.
Bits of black paint are flaking off,
where the motorcycles roar, around and around,
rising higher on the silo walls,
the bodies bent toward the horizon,
driven by angry women dressed in black.

I know that books are tired of us.
I know they are chaining the Bible to chairs.
Books don't want to remain in the same room with us anymore.

New Testaments are escaping! . . . Dressed as women . . . they go
off after dark.
And Plato! Plato . . . Plato wants to go backwards . . .
He wants to hurry back up the river of time, so he can end up as
some blob of seaflesh rotting on an Australian beach.

V

Why are they dying? I have written this so many times.
They are dying because the President has opened a Bible again.

They are dying because gold deposits have been found among the
Shoshoni indians.

Because money follows intellect!
and intellect is like a fan opening in the wind—

The marines think that unless they die the rivers will not move.
They are dying so that mountain shadows can fall north in the
afternoon,
so that the beetle can move along the ground near the fallen twigs.

VI

But if one of those children came near that we have set on fire,
came toward you like a grey barn, walking,
you would howl like a wind tunnel in a hurricane,
you would tear at your shirt with blue hands,
you would drive over your own child's wagon trying to back up,
the pupils of your eyes would go wild—

If a child came by burning, you would dance on a lawn,
trying to walk into the air, digging into your cheeks,
you would ram your head against the wall of your bedroom
like a bull penned too long in his moody pen—

If one of those children came toward me with both hands
in the air, fire rising along both elbows,
I would suddenly go back to my animal brain,
I would drop on all fours, screaming,

my vocal chords would turn blue, yours would too,
it would be two days before I could play with my own
    children again.

VII

I want to sleep awhile in the rays of the sun slanting over
    the snow.
Don't wake me.
Don't tell me how much grief there is in the leaf with its
    natural oils.
Don't tell me how many children have been born with stumpy feet
all those years we lived in Augustine's shadow.
Tell me about the dust that falls from the yellow daffodil shaken
    in the restless winds.
Tell me about the particles of Babylonian thought that still pass
    through the earthworm every day.
Don't tell me about "the frightening labourers who do not
    read books."

Now the whole nation starts to whirl,
the end of the Republic breaks off,
Europe comes to take revenge,
the mad beast covered with European hair rushes through the
    mesa bushes in Mendocino County,
pigs rush toward the cliff,
the waters underneath part: in one ocean luminous globes float up
    (in them hairy and ecstatic rock musicians)—
in the other, the teeth-mother, naked at last.

Let us drive cars
up
the light beams
to the stars . . . .

And yet return to earth crouched inside the drop of sweat
that falls again and again
from the chin of the Protestant tied in the fire.

Philip Jones Griffiths

It must never be forgotten that despite the Madison Avenue talk of "Winning Hearts and Minds" the chief characteristic of the American involvement was the endeavour to slaughter and maim the greatest number of Vietnamese.

Here are some pictures of those that suffered. The war has been won by the people. We must never be allowed to forget at what cost.

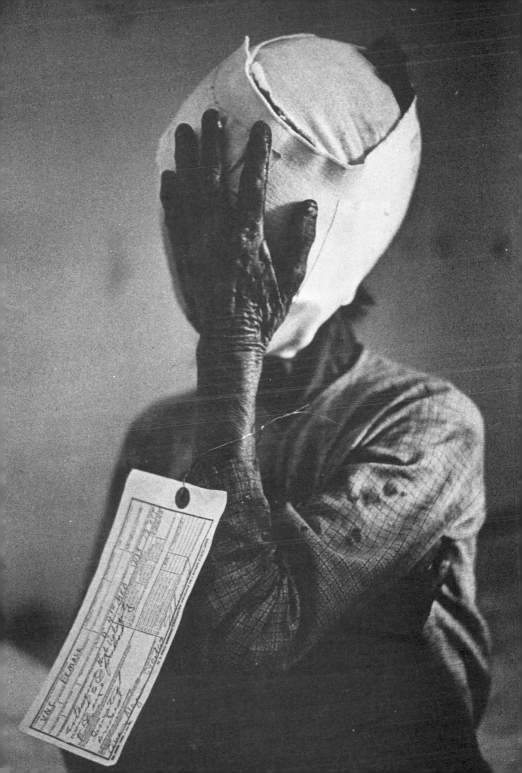

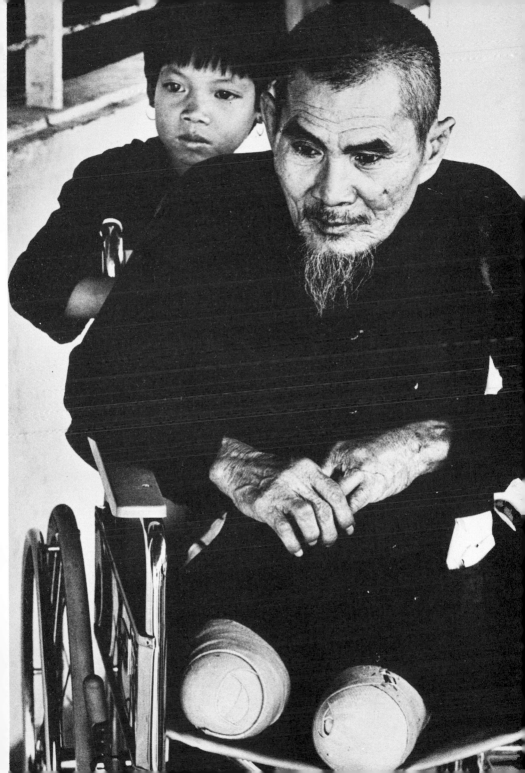

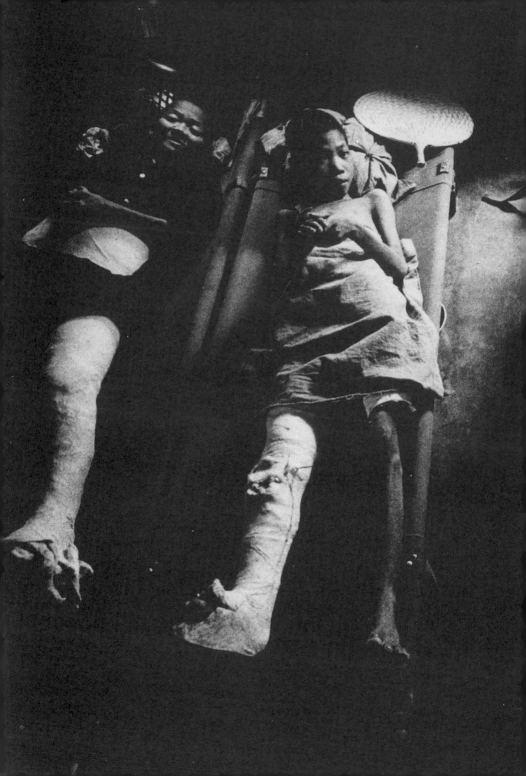

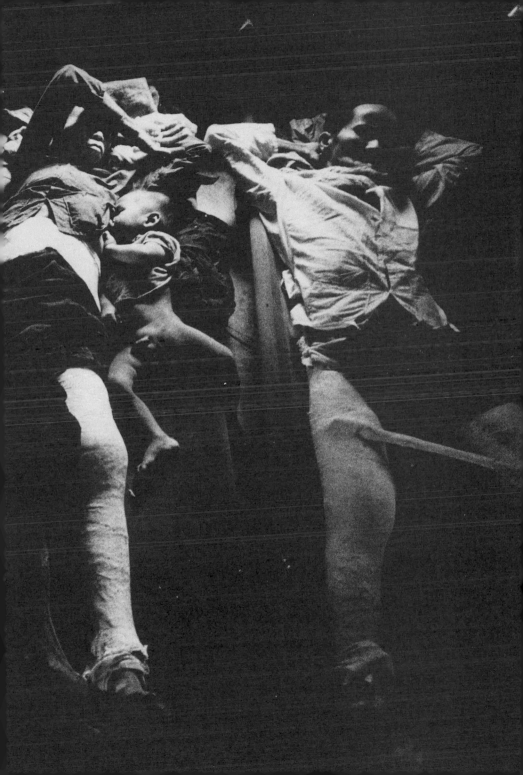

The Land That is Ours
Nam Ha

At last I have finished digging my shelter. Without doubt it has been the most troublesome dugout I have made since I learnt to dig and to shoot.

I throw myself on the cold earth, my back against the trunk of a tree, arms crossed on my knees, breathing like a blacksmith's bellows. Somewhere in our sector firing breaks out wildly for a moment like hard dry barking in the distance, then ceases. I listen attentively waiting for it to start up again, but the silence is complete.

"Well, the job is done," I say to myself, looking at the sky. Overhead the trees are woven into the form of a light dome. The pale light of the last distant fires left by enemy planes begins to melt in the first vague light of dawn.

I become aware at that moment of the tired snorting in the distance of a heavy transport plane, with its paunchy silhouette it is the one we call the "seed bearer" and sometimes the "dragonfly."

Gradually the sky grows lighter. The forest exhales a vapour which clings about the tree tops, stretching out in a thick sheet. I reckon that with this kind of mist the planes will be prevented from going about their foul business for at least an hour; so, knife in hand, I go in search of suitable branches to roof my dugout. Presently I come back from the forest with a load of the right kind of branches for the job.

In their horseshoe formation round about me the other comrades of our company are already hard at work roofing their dugouts. The earth hereabouts is really tough, but all the same I have nearly finished the perfect hide. I arrange the branches firmly around the entrance. I pile earth over the roofing branches, and camouflage the whole thing with leaves.

In a few minutes the roofing is finished and I look at it at ease, wiping my muddy hands on my trousers.

From my cartridge bag I pull out a rag saturated with oil to clean my rifle. Then I prepare my ammunition and polish up my bayonet.

I hold the stock of my rifle against my jaw, the dew that has formed on it tingles through my blood with a delicious freshness. I lean the gun against a tree and rummage in my haversack for cartridges to fill up my belt, and take out a little tobacco to roll. Tearing a page from my notebook I wrap it carefully and put it in my shirt sleeve for a future smoke. Then, having buckled up my haversack I put it by the entrance of the dugout with my rifle across the top.

There is nothing more to be done but to take care of my stomach with half a bowl of rice washed down with a swig of water, then perhaps to crown it, a few drags at a home-made cigarette. After this I am ready to fight and if necessary to go on fighting all day till the coming of darkness.

Thin trails of vapour detach themselves and float into the sky, gradually collecting and thickening into a mass. The first rays of the sun, thin and pointed like needles of light, pierce the mists with sparkling threads. A wagtail poised on a twig opens his beak to breathe in the freshness of morning, he begins to sing, bobbing his pretty tail up and down as though to beat the measure.

In the strange morning stillness that broods over this battle area like a spell, the song of the bird sounds to me like a fountain of clear water.

Huyinh in his dugout next to mine screws up his eyes to admire the little singer. Quang, our group leader, is the next to raise his head and soon everyone in Group 7 is looking at the wagtail.

But not for long. Quang gathers us all round the roots of a huge old tree with thick foliage to brief us for the day.

"I have had a look at the dugouts," he says. "On the whole they are fine, though perhaps the camouflage is not as perfect as it might be. The news is that a neighbouring unit has wiped out the enemy in their subsector. One group has even seized an armoured car which they immediately turned to use by training the machine gun in it against the enemy planes. Today it is our turn. We must try to emulate our brothers. We can wipe out the force that is going to be sent against us!"

The wagtail continues to sing in the tree. Quang, after a glance towards it, continues, "Go and finish making the camouflage perfect. Then have a bite to eat and afterwards its everyone to his burrow. The comrade on observation must also remain in his dugout and keep well hidden."

He picks us for observation, Huyinh and me, to keep watch in turn.

We return to our dugouts to put the finishing touches to our camouflage and then bring out our rice bowls. I have hardly swallowed my breakfast before the shriek of a jet plane tears the serenity of the sky. Huyinh wipes his hands on his trousers, grumbling, "The bastards, they're arriving already." Then turning to me, "Hi, Son, which of us is on duty first . . . . shall I? Right? Get into your hole, when I chuck a clod at you, come and relieve me. Right?"

I nod in agreement and uncork my water jar to swallow a

mouthful of water. The planes have already completed their second circle round our sky.

Above the tree tops in front of us the troop carrier "dragon-fly", labouring and groaning, its legs dangling, searches for a place to make a landing where it may disgorge its troops. Now the fighter planes descending in closer circles rend the air with their frenzied thumping just above our heads. "Always on the same trail!" I remark to myself, and decide to ignore them as far as possible for the moment.

The troop carrier changes direction and makes as though to come towards our sector. I draw together the leaves of my camouflage and crouch in my shelter, determined to make myself as comfortable as possible while I wait, keeping my gun ready. I uncover the grenades, arrange them within grabbing distance and sit listening. The jets descending with their shattering air disturbance seem to be about to tear the roofs off our dugouts and even to uproot the forest trees. A powerful gust throws into my den a lively blast of cool air and the branch that camouflages the entrance is shaken as in a storm. In spite of this rough treatment an irresistible need to sleep takes possession of me and I am beginning to nod when my head bashes on the wall of the dugout. I wake up completely to realise that bombs are falling quite close, the explosions are at ground level. Each explosion sucks me up and then thumps me down again. The dugout seems to be cracking in the pressure of the blast. I feel like somebody in a small boat tossing helplessly in a stormy sea. The earth shakes violently like a hammock, as for my roof it seems to be turning upside down, and the explosions are so loud they are enough to burst your eardrums. Behind me I hear the tree on which the wagtail was singing come tearing down. Where has he taken refuge, poor thing? — after singing so delightfully to the peaceful morning.

After the explosives comes the napalm. Heavy concussions echo all round our sector. An acrid smell of burning chemical comes into the dugout and I am aware that fire is spreading outside. I take my towel, soak it with water from the jar as a precaution against toxic gasses.

After the napalm the low level strafing — the shattering clatter of the 20mm machine gun tears the air.

Propped against the wall of my dugout I take from my sleeve my bit of tobacco for a smoke. The bullets dance ineffectively off my good roof. All they can do is to plough it up a bit on the surface. I draw in long drags of tobacco, swallowing the smoke. The smoke seems to fire my blood. I feel urged to throw off the cover and jump out, but you must be patient. You have to wait. The enemy is making preparations for landing. He has hardly finished the preliminary attack, there will be two more before he dares to disembark his troops.

At this rate I still have some considerable time to cramp my bottom in this den. I begin to get tired. It is definitely a change from the night's activity, when I had to make the best of every flare from the horizon to dig my shelter. This night devoted entirely to digging has been unique in my life as a fighter. The spade that I used seemed to make little impression on this obstinate soil, but if I was forced to make a grimace with every effort at the same time a memory was being carved in my mind. I look at my handiwork. Why not admit it, it is a tremendous work, this which cost me twelve solid hours of struggle. In the course of the night I have to admit that at one point I became a prey to discouragement and irritation, so unyielding was that earth. But thoughts of the intensity of the fighting in this sector spurred me on. And now, look how gallantly this hole resists bombs, fire, bullets and all. I put out my hand to stroke the layers of hard earth and the chill of it against the palm shivers through my whole body. I laugh to myself exploring with my finger the close knit flesh of this earth.

A curious thought occurs to me; I cut on the wall with the point of my knife the number 200. Yes, this is it, my two hundredth individual dugout. In addition to those two hundred there are also about fifty in different places which I have dug for the people there, besides a hundred or so rough holes that I have hastily scraped for shelter in battlefields up and down the country. I have spent hours standing, sitting, lying, sleeping, in hundreds of shelters carved out of hundreds of different soils . . . . but at this point a series of bombs exploding all round the dugout interrupts my thoughts. A handful of mud lands against the entrance, does this mean Huyinh is calling me to relieve him? I stuff a couple of grenades into my trouser pockets, take my gun and climb up to the opening. I stop to listen carefully for the sound of falling bombs in order to judge from what height they are dropping. Then I come out. The sunlight hits me bang in the eyes and completely dazzles me for a moment. Seeing my head appear, Huyinh shouts out, "Hello, what are you up to?"

"Coming to relieve you."

"But I haven't called you yet."

Huyinh is pulling out a piece of gauze from his belt. I screw up my eyes to see why.

"Are you wounded?"

Huyinh nods his head, holding out his left hand.

"They've done me out of a bit of flesh." As he speaks he wraps the wound.

"A spot of mercurochrome will fix it."

"Oh yes," he grins.

"Get into your hole. I'll take over. They're only at the second round. There'll be more before they dare to land troops."

Huyinh disappears into his dugout. I take a comprehensive look at the positions of my section. Everywhere there are bomb craters, a bomb has even fallen just beside the roof of my dugout. Ruined trees sprawl on the ground, smoke still mounts skyward in thick columns. But I can see that every shelter is intact and I am overjoyed. I screw up my eyes to watch the antics of the planes in the sky. They are increasing altitude, but from the direction of the morning sun a wedge formation of fighter bombers comes bursting through a chasm between two clouds. They look as though they were blackened with smoke. This is the third wave. The planes describe a circle and turn close in with the object of dropping bombs on our positions. Down come the bombs with their pointed muzzles as black as coal. The explosions shake the ground with violent convulsions. They seem to be trying to tear me out of the earth. I spread out my limbs and hang on like a spider to the wall of my dugout. When the explosions cease I wipe my face. I am all covered with mud. I tap the walls of the hide to test them for damage. A large lizard and part of the roof come tumbling in. I hardly have time to duck before a black object belching smoke passes my face at great speed and a violent explosion bursts in front of me. Again the blast just about blows me clean out of the dugout. But not quite. I remain firmly embedded in the bosom of the earth. If I hadn't taken the trouble to make a dugout of such monumental solidity, that really would have been the end of me! Yes, I have made two hundred dugouts in two hundred different places; near the sea where the soil is sandy, in the plains of the West and of the interior where the land is limestone, in districts where the alluvial clay soil yields easily to the spade. Then there are lands where the soil is red such as in the coffee and rubber growing areas of the East and there is the laterite earth that is formed along the eroded banks of some rivers.

From every place where I have fought, from every earth in which I have dug myself a shelter, I have stored up some special memory. Among these memories, for instance, there is one of the region of Gia Dinh. It was there that I celebrated the New Year once with my own countrymen during a series of actions designed to resist the "search and destroy" operations of the enemy. During the days of that campaign I dug shelters and fought alongside a young girl partisan and soon after we decided to get married.

Well, this is the way I have lived.

As for this place in which I find myself today, what shall I say of it? It was completely unknown to me, very far away, and I would never have guessed that anything would have brought me here. But the designs of the military stategy have led me here and it only needs one night for me to find that already it has become my home. It is no longer foreign to me, it has become the same stuff as my own flesh and blood. It has received in its body the bombs and bullets that were intended for me, it has undergone the most terrible trials to protect me. It is my mother and I am its child — a soldier of earth.

In another moment the American planes will be here to discharge their cargo of soldiers and I shall rise out of the earth to wipe out the enemy — here, on the very soil where they land. I shall rise to protect our earth from their pollution.

The bombers have disappeared. The "dragonfly" is flying in diminishing circles preparing to land. A lump of earth hits me on the back. Turning I see Quang, our chief, hiding behind a tree. "We have information," he says, "that the enemy is about to land in front of our positions. We must give them a good reception. Anything new, Son, since the morning? No disasters to the dugouts? By God we must thank our good earth for its protection. It was a bit hot at one point, wasn't it? Pass on orders to Huyinh, will you." I flick a piece of mud into Huyinh's dugout. He appears at once and I pass on the orders of the chief.

A new wave of fighter bombers now appears, descends and comes swooping in to drop their bombs. I make a dive for my dugout but don't have enough time to pull my hand in from the entrance when a bomb explodes immediately behind me. There is suddenly an intense cold in my left hand. I draw it in and look — my little finger hangs by a string of flesh. I sever it with a sudden tug and tie a bandage round the hand. The planes having relieved themselves of their bombs give the area a "blind" strafing with their machine guns, then climb the air and roar off again. Immediately from the East the choppers appear once more. They fly in groups of three looking like fat flies. The sky echoes with their din, the air trembles and vibrates. The first helicopter flying at treetop level drops some kind of object from which pours a reddish smoke. "This is it, now we're getting the lot," I mutter.

The "dragonfly" has not succeeded in discovering the presence of hundreds of armed men who, hidden in the earth, have arranged a trap which is about to close.

I stoop to get my haversack on my back, set the grenades at the entrance of the dugout, carefully load my gun and prepare my bayonet. I pull down the scorched branches that conceal the hide, and I wait . . . . .

The first group of helicopters is approaching. Already I can see the enemy figures in their green get-up. The helicopters are no more than five metres from the ground.

The three of them pass before my eyes a stone's throw away. The men drop their grenades and then jump to land.

They fall, some on their backs, some face downwards, some jump with their legs all flying. I reckon I am about fifteen metres from the one that has fallen nearest to me. I watch them form themselves three deep. They just about make up a company. The American "advisors" after getting painfully to their feet are staggering like drunks, nevertheless they show the arrogance of men who do not doubt that they are advancing upon firm ground. No doubt they are thinking to themselves that all their bombs must have annihilated any "Vietcong" that might have been lurking about here.

Looking at them I feel my blood fire up. My whole being quivers with the tension of a drawn bowstring. I clench my teeth, firmly clutch my first grenade, bringing my arm back for the throw. Moments pass, indescribable moments. I hear the three mines of our sappers go off and at once I fling my first grenade at the nearest section of the enemy. Before it bursts I follow it with another. The two explode very nearly at the same moment.

Our group, followed immediately by the whole company, opens fire from the dugouts. It is the moment to close the trap. Grenades rain down on the enemy formations, breaking them up. Our machine gun, manned by comrade Chi, sweeps the ground mowing down the enemy, who take flight on all fours bellowing like cattle. I spot a Yankee officer who is wriggling away in the grass. His legs appear at the end of my sights. I press the trigger, The Yankee kicks frantically then lies still.

Now from behind our lines the bugle sounds the assault. I leap from my dugout. Our leader Quang with Huyinh and another comrade rake the area with a spray of bullets from their sub-machine guns.

Our enemies, paralysed, remain rooted to the spot then drop to the ground. Some put up a futile return fire. Some fly in panic or holding up their arms stand like leaves in the wind. They cannot recover their senses after the shock of our surprise attack, it is clear they do not quite understand what has happened.

Our company spreads over the battle area like the waves of the Mekong at the time of floodwater.

The battle is as brief and violent as a tropical storm. It rages for not more than twelve minutes, then once more silence takes over, broken only by the groans of the wounded and by the distant rumbling of aircraft.

The sun is high by this time. A dazzling heat beats off the scorched ground, enough to burn your feet. The heat of the earth is like an oven about the dead strewn on the battlefield, the blood begins to turn thick and black.

With other comrades it is my business to guard the prisoners and await the arrival of the detachment who are to come and relieve us of the charge. We wait there from noon until the evening. From the battle area we hear the distant sound of firing. At four o'clock the convoy appears. They have been lost in the forest.

As soon as we have completed the hand-over of prisoners I return to the scene of the fighting. Several times on the way there I am held up by bombs so that it is not until nightfall that I finally reach my unit. I report on my duty and then return to my position. There I find Huyinh eating his supper.

"Has there been any fighting while I was away?" I ask. He shakes his head.

"Then how is it I heard so much firing?"

"The comrades of the next unit."

"Has there been bombing here?"

"Too right there has!" and Huyinh points out several new craters. "They have their revenge — huh?"

I look around. The appearance of that part of the forest is completely changed since the morning. The bombs have broken or uprooted every tree and ploughed great wounds in the earth. After a silence I ask Huyinh, "And our unit — have we lost any?" He shakes his head.

It takes me some time to find my dugout. Three new bomb craters have been opened here which brings the number to six in my immediate vicinity. I stoop to examine my hide and am surprised to see that whereas the entrance as I dug it had been rectangular, it is now quite round. I jump in, stumble on fallen clods of earth and feel about to see if the walls are still sound. Nothing serious that a little repairing won't put right, the main structure is still good and solid.

I clamber out again in response to a summons from our leader who it appears is giving the order to march. Seeing that I am a bit slow to get his meaning he explains, "We must move on again and make preparations for another bout somewhere else. There will always be more of this sort of thing."

So our unit is moving off to march towards a new destination. I am going to make the acquaintance of another piece of my native land. There I will dig my two-hundred-and-first shelter, and when I have done it, that piece of earth which now is quite strange to me will become my flesh and my blood, protecting me, guarding my life.

(Translated by Mary Cowan).

King Henry
Pete Seeger

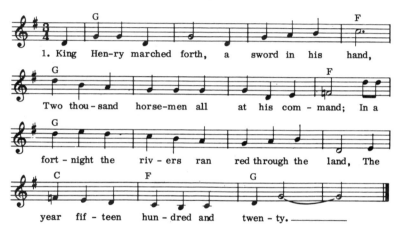

1. King Hen-ry marched forth, a sword in his hand,
Two thou-sand horse-men all at his com - mand; In a
fort - night the riv - ers ran red through the land, The
year fif - teen hun - dred and twen - ty.

© Copyright 1965 by FALL RIVER MUSIC Inc.,

King Henry marched forth, a sword in his hand,
Two thousand horsemen all at his command;
In a fortnight the rivers ran red through the land,
The year fifteen hundred and twenty.

The year it is now much later, it seems,
It's easier far in the land of our dreams;
Just keep your mouth shut and don't hear the screams,
Ten thousand miles over the ocean.

Simon was drafted in 'sixty-three,
In 'sixty-four, sent over the sea;
Last month this letter he sent to me,
He said, "You won't like what I'm saying."

He said, "We've no friends here, not hardly a one,
We've got a few generals who just want our guns;
But it'll take more than them if we're ever to win,
Why, we'll have to flatten the country."

"It's my own troops I have to watch out for," he said,
"I sleep with a pistol right under my head;"
He wrote this last month, last week he was dead,
His body shipped home in a casket.*

I mind my own business, I watch my TV,
Complain about taxes, but pay anyway;
In a civilized manner my forefathers betray,
Who long ago struggled for freedom.

But each day a new headline screams at my bluff,
On TV some general says we must be tough;
In my dreams I stare at this family I love,
All gutted and spattered with napalm.

King Henry marched forth, a sword in his hand,
Two thousand horsemen all at his command;
In a fortnight the rivers ran red through the land,
Ten thousand miles over the ocean.

*The quote in the fifth verse is from an actual letter from a
   US 'adviser' to his wife, a week before he was killed in Vietnam.

Waist Deep in the Big Muddy

It was back in nine-teen for-ty two, I was a mem-ber of a good pla-toon. We were on ma-neuvers in a-Loo-zi-an-na, one night by the light of the moon. The cap-tain told us to ford a ri-ver That's how it all be-gun. We were knee deep in the Big Mud-dy but the big fool said to push on. (2. The)

© Copyright 1967 MELODY TRAILS Inc., New York, N.Y.

It was back in nineteen forty two,
I was a member of a good platoon.
We were on maneuvers in a Loozianna,
One night by the light of the moon.
   The captain told us to ford a river
   That's how it all begun.
   We were knee deep in the big Muddy
   But the big fool said to push on.

The sergeant said, "Sir, are you sure,
This is the best way back to the base?"
"Sergeant, go on; I forded this river
'Bout a mile above this place
   It'll be a little soggy but just keep slogging.
   We'll soon be on dry ground."
   We were waist deep in the Big Muddy
   And the big fool said to push on.

The sergeant said, "Sir, with all this equipment
No man'll be able to swim."
"Sergeant, don't be a nervous Nellie,"
The Captain said to him.
   "All we need is a little determination;
   Men, follow me, I'll lead on."
   We were neck deep in the Big Muddy
   And the big fool said to push on.

All at once, the moon clouded over,
We heard a gurgling cry.
A few seconds later, the Captain's helmet
Was all that floated by.
   The sergeant said, "Turn around men,
   I'm in charge from now on."
   And we just made it out of the Big Muddy
   With the Captain dead and gone.

We stripped and dived and found his body
Stuck in the old quicksand
I guess he didn't know that the water was deeper
Than the place he'd once before been.
   Another stream had joined the Big Muddy
   'Bout a half mile from where we'd gone.
   We were lucky to escape from the Big Muddy
   When the big fool said to push on.

Well, I'm not gonna point any moral;

I'll leave that for yourself
Maybe you're still walking and you're still talking
And you'd like to keep your health.
　　But every time I read the papers
　　That old feeling comes on;
　　We're waist deep in the Big Muddy
　　And the big fool says to push on.

Waist deep in the Big Muddy
And the big fool says to push on
Waist deep in the Big Muddy
And the big fool says to push on
　　Waist deep! Neck deep!
　　Soon even a tall man'll be over his head
　　Waist deep in the Big Muddy!
　　And the big fool says to push on!

The Gutless Wonder
Kurt Vonnegut and
Philip Jones Griffiths

Billy Pilgrim opened his eyes in the hospital in Vermont, did not know where he was. Watching him was his son, Robert. Robert was wearing the uniform of the famous Green Berets. Robert's hair was short, was wheat-colored bristles. Robert was clean and neat. He was decorated with a Purple Heart and a Silver Star and a Bronze Star with two clusters.

This was a boy who had flunked out of high school, who had been an alcoholic at sixteen, who had run with a rotten bunch of kids, who had been arrested for tipping over hundreds of tombstones in a Catholic cemetery one time. He was all straightened out now. His posture was wonderful and his shoes were shined and his trousers were pressed, and he was a leader of men.

'Dad?'

Billy Pilgrim closed his eyes again.

THE GUTLESS WONDER was the title of a book by Kilgore Trout. It was about a robot who had bad breath, who became popular after his halitosis was cured. But what made the story remarkable, since it was written in 1932, was that it predicted the widespread use of burning jellied gasoline on human beings.

It was dropped on them from airplanes. Robots did the dropping. They had no conscience, and no circuits which would allow them to imagine what was happening to the people on the ground.

Trout's leading robot looked like a human being, and could talk and dance and so on, and go out with girls. And nobody held it against him that he dropped jellied gasoline on people. But they found his halitosis unforgivable. But then he cleared that up, and he was welcomed to the human race.

The speaker at the Lions Club meeting was a major in the Marines. He said that Americans had no choice but to keep fighting in Vietnam until they achieved victory or until the Communists realised that they could not force their way of life on weak countries. The major had been there on two separate tours of duty. He told of many terrible and many wonderful things he had seen. He was in favour of increased bombings, of bombing North Vietnam back into the Stone Age, if it refused to see reason.

Billy was not moved to protest the bombing of North Vietnam, did not shudder about the hideous things he himself had seen bombing do. He was simply having lunch with the Lions Club, of which he was past president.

Billy had a framed prayer on his office wall which expressed his method for keeping going, even though he was unenthusiastic about living. A lot of patients who saw the prayer on Billy's wall told him that it helped *them* to keep going, too. It went like this

GOD GRANT ME
THE SERENITY TO ACCEPT
THE THINGS I CANNOT CHANGE,
COURAGE
TO CHANGE THE THINGS I CAN,
AND WISDOM ALWAYS
TO TELL THE
DIFFERENCE.

Among the things Billy Pilgrim could not change were the past, the present and the future.

She had lost her husband, Robert, in a war in Vietnam. He was a graduate of West Point, a military academy which turned young men into homicidal maniacs for use in war. Robert was sent to Vietnam. He was shipped home in a plastic body bag.

They rode in silence for a while, and then the driver made another good point. He said he knew that his truck was turning the atmosphere into poison gas, and that the planet was being turned into pavement so his truck could go anywhere. "So I'm committing suicide," he said.

"Don't worry about it," said Trout.

"My brother is even worse," the driver went on. "He works in a factory that makes chemicals for killing plants and trees in Vietnam." Vietnam was a country where America was trying to make people stop being Communists by dropping things on them from airplanes. The chemicals he mentioned were intended to kill all the foliage, so it would be harder for the Communists to hide from airplanes.

"Don't worry about it," said Trout.

"In the long run, *he's* committing suicide," said the driver. "Seems like the only kind of job an American can get these days is committing suicide in some way."

"Good point," said Trout.

Where Have You Gone, Charming Billy?

Tim O'Brien

The platoon of twenty-six soldiers moved slowly in the dark, single file, not talking. One by one, like sheep in a dream, they passed through the hedgerow, crossed quietly over a meadow and came down to the rice paddy. There they stopped. Their leader knelt down, motioning with his hand, and one by one the other soldiers squatted in the shadows, vanishing in the primitive stealth of warfare. For a long time they did not move. Except for the sounds of their breathing, and once a soft, fluid trickle as one of them urinated, the twenty-six men were very quiet: some of them excited by the adventure, some of them afraid, some of them exhausted from the long night march, some of them looking forward to reaching the sea where they would be safe. At the rear of the column, Private First Class Paul Berlin lay quietly with his forehead resting on the black plastic stock of his rifle, his eyes closed. He was pretending he was not in the war, pretending he had not watched Billy Boy Watkins die of a heart attack that afternoon. He was pretending he was a boy again, camping with his father in the midnight summer along the Des Moines River. In the dark, with his eyes pinched shut, he pretended. He pretended that when he opened his eyes, his father would be there by the campfire and they would talk softly about whatever came to mind and then roll into their sleeping bags, and that later they'd wake up and it would be morning and there would not be a war, and that Billy Boy Watkins had not died of a heart attack that afternoon. He pretended he was not a soldier.

In the morning, when they reached the sea, it would be better. The hot afternoon would be over, he would bathe in the sea and he would forget how frightened he had been on his first day at the war. The second day would not be so bad. He would learn.

There was a sound beside him, a movement and then a breathed: "Hey!"

He opened his eyes, shivering as if emerging from a deep nightmare.

"Hey!" a shadow whispered. "We're *moving*, for Chrissake. Get up."

"Okay."

"You sleepin', or something?"

"No." He could not make out the soldier's face. With clumsy, concrete hands he clawed for his rifle, found it, found his helmet.

The soldier-shadow grunted. "You got a lot to learn, buddy. I'd shoot you if I thought you was sleepin'. Let's go."

Private First Class Paul Berlin blinked.

Ahead of him, silhouetted against the sky, he saw the string of soldiers wading into the flat paddy, the blue outline of their shoulders and packs and weapons. He was comfortable. He did not want to move. But he was afraid, for it was his first night at the war, so he hurried to catch up, stumbling once, scraping his knee, groping as though blind; his boots sank into the thick paddy water and he smelled it all around him. He would tell his mother how it smelled: mud and algae and cattle manure and chlorophyll, decay, breeding mosquitoes and leeches as big as mice, the fecund warmth of the paddy waters rising up to his cut knee. But he would not tell how frightened he had been.

Once they reached the sea, things would be better. They would have their rear guarded by three thousand miles of ocean, and they would swim and dive into the breakers and hunt crayfish and smell the salt, and they would be safe.

He followed the shadow of the man in front of him. It was a clear night. Already the Southern Cross was out. And other stars he could not yet name—soon, he thought, he would learn their names. And puffy night clouds. There was not yet a moon. Wading through the paddy, his boots made sleepy, sloshing sounds, like a lullaby, and he tried not to think. Though he was afraid, he now knew that fear came in many degrees and types and peculiar categories, and he knew that his fear now was not so bad as it had been in the hot afternoon, when poor Billy Boy Watkins got killed by a heart attack. His fear now was diffuse and unformed: ghosts in the tree line, nighttime fears of a child, a boogieman in the closet that his father would open to show empty, saying, "See? Nothing there, champ. Now you can sleep." In the afternoon it had been worse; the fear had been bundled and tight and he'd been on his hands and knees, crawling like an insect, an ant escaping a giant's footsteps and thinking nothing, brain flopping and thinking nothing at all, watching while Billy Boy Watkins died.

Now as he stepped out of the paddy onto a narrow dirt path, now the fear was mostly the fear of being so terribly afraid again.

He tried not to think.

There were tricks he'd learned to keep from thinking. Counting: He counted his steps, concentrating on the numbers, pretending that the numbers were dollar bills and that each step through the night made him richer and richer, so that soon he would become a wealthy man, and he kept counting and considered the ways he might spend the money after the war and what he would do. He would look his father in the eye and shrug and say, "It was pretty bad at first, but I learned a lot and I got used to it." Then he would tell his father the story of Billy Boy Watkins. But he would never let on how frightened he had been. "Not so bad," he would say instead, making his father feel proud.

Songs, another trick to stop from thinking: *Where have you gone, Billy Boy, Billy Boy, oh, where have you gone, charming Billy? I have gone to seek a wife, she's the joy of my life, but she's a young thing and cannot leave her mother,* and other songs that he sang in his thoughts as he walked toward the sea. And when he reached the sea he would dig a deep hole in the sand and he would sleep like the high clouds, and he would not be afraid any more.

The moon came out. Pale and shrunken to the size of a dime.

The helmet was heavy on his head. In the morning he would adjust the leather binding. He would clean his rifle, too. Even though he had been frightened to shoot it during the hot afternoon, he would carefully clean the breech and the muzzle and the ammunition so that next time he would be ready and not so afraid. In the morning, when they reached the sea, he would begin to make friends with some of the other soldiers. He would learn their names and laugh at their jokes. Then when the war was over he would write to them once in a while and exchange memories.

Walking, sleeping in his walking, he felt better. He watched the moon come higher.

Once they skirted a sleeping village. The smells again— straw, cattle, mildew. The men were quiet. On the far side of the village, buried in the dark smells, a dog barked. The column stopped until the barking died away; then they marched fast away from the village, through a graveyard filled with conical-shaped burial mounds and tiny altars made of clay and stone. The grave-yard had a perfumy smell. A nice place to spend the night, he thought. The mounds would make fine battlements, and the smell was nice and the place was quiet. But they went on, passing through a hedgerow and across another paddy and east toward the sea.

He walked carefully. He remembered what he'd been taught: Stay off the center of the path, for that was where the land mines and booby traps were planted, where stupid and lazy soldiers like to walk. Stay alert, he'd been taught. Better alert than inert. Ag-ile, mo-bile, hos-tile. He wished he'd paid better attention to the training. He could not remember what they'd said about how to stop being afraid; they hadn't given any lessons in courage—not that he could remember—and they hadn't men-tioned how Billy Boy Watkins would die of a heart attack, his face turning pale and the veins popping out.

Private First Class Paul Berlin walked carefully.

Stretching ahead of him like dark beads on an invisible chain, the string of shadow-soldiers whose names he did not yet know moved with the silence and slow grace of smoke. Now and again moonlight was reflected off a machine gun or a wrist watch. But mostly the soldiers were quiet and hidden and far-away-seeming in a peaceful night, strangers on a long street, and he felt quite separate from them, as if trailing behind like the caboose on a night train, pulled along by inertia, sleepwalking, an afterthought to the war.

So he walked carefully, counting his steps. When he had counted to three thousand four hundred and eighty-five, the column stopped.

One by one the soldiers knelt or squatted down.

The grass along the path was wet. Private First Class Paul Berlin lay back and turned his head so that he could lick at the dew with his eyes closed, another trick to forget the war. He might have slept. "I *wasn't* afraid," he was screaming or dreaming, facing his father's stern eyes. "I wasn't afraid," he was saying. When he opened his eyes, a soldier was sitting beside him, quietly chewing a stick of Doublemint gum.

"You sleepin' again?" the soldier whispered.

"No," said Private First Class Paul Berlin. "Hell, no."

The soldier grunted, chewing his gum. Then he twisted the cap off his canteen, took a swallow and handed it through the dark.

"Take some," he whispered.

"Thanks."

"You're the new guy?"

"Yes." He did not want to admit it, being new to the war.

The soldier grunted and handed him a stick of gum. "Chew it quiet—okay? Don't blow no bubbles or nothing."

"Thanks. I won't." He could not make out the man's face in the shadows.

They sat still and Private First Class Paul Berlin chewed the gum until all the sugars were gone; then the soldier said, "Bad day today, buddy."

Private First Class Paul Berlin nodded wisely, but he did not speak.

"Don't think it's always so bad," the soldier whispered. "I don't wanna scare you. You'll get used to it soon enough. . . . . They been fighting wars a long time, and you get used to it."

"Yeah."

"You will."

They were quiet awhile. And the night was quiet, no crickets or birds, and it was hard to imagine it was truly a war. He searched for the soldier's face but could not find it. It did not matter much. Even if he saw the fellow's face, he would not know the name; and even if he knew the name, it would not matter much.

"Haven't got the time?" the soldier whispered.

"No."

"Rats . . . . Don't matter, really. Goes faster if you don't know the time, anyhow."

"Sure."

"What's your name, buddy?"

"Paul."

"Nice to meet ya," he said, and in the dark beside the path they shook hands. "Mine's Toby. Everybody calls me Buffalo, though." The soldier's hand was strangely warm and soft. But it was a very big hand. "Sometimes they just call me Buff," he said.

And again they were quiet. They lay in the grass and waited. The moon was very high now and very bright, and they were waiting for cloud cover.

The soldier suddenly snorted.

"What is it?"

"Nothin'," he said, but then he snorted again. "A bloody *heart attack!*" the soldier said. "Can't get over it—old Billy Boy croaking from a lousy heart attack . . . . A heart attack—can you believe it?"

The idea of it made Private First Class Paul Berlin smile. He couldn't help it.

"Ever hear of such a thing?"

"Not till now," said Private First Class Paul Berlin, still smiling.

"Me neither," said the soldier in the dark. "Gawd, dying of a heart attack. Didn't know him, did you."

"No."

"Tough as nails."

"Yeah."

"And what happens? A heart attack. Can you imagine it?"

"Yes," said Private First Class Paul Berlin. He wanted to laugh. "I can imagine it." And he imagined it clearly. He giggled —he couldn't help it. He imagined Billy's father opening the telegram: SORRY TO INFORM YOU THAT YOUR SON BILLY BOY WAS YESTERDAY SCARED TO DEATH IN ACTION IN THE REPUBLIC OF VIETNAM, VALIANTLY SUCCUMBING TO A HEART ATTACK SUFFERED WHILE UNDER ENORMOUS STRESS; AND IT IS WITH GREATEST SYMPATHY THAT . . . . He giggled again. He rolled onto his belly and pressed his face into his arms. His body was shaking with giggles.

The big soldier hissed at him to shut up, but he could not

stop giggling and remembering the hot afternoon, and poor Billy Boy, and how they'd been drinking Coca-Cola from bright-red aluminium cans, and how they'd started on the day's march, and how a little while later poor Billy Boy stepped on the mine, and how it made a tiny little sound—*poof*—and how Billy Boy stood there with his mouth wide-open, looking down at where his foot had been blown off, and how finally Billy Boy sat down very casually, not saying a word, with his foot lying behind him, most of it still in the boot.

He giggled louder—he could not stop. He bit his arm, trying to stifle it, but remembering: "War's over, Billy," the men had said in consolation, but Billy Boy got scared and started crying and said he was about to die. "Nonsense," the medic said, Doc Peret, but Billy Boy kept bawling, tightening up, his face going pale and transparent and his veins popping out. Scared stiff. Even when Doc Peret stuck him with morphine, Billy Boy kept crying.

"Shut up!" the big soldier hissed, but Private First Class Paul Berlin could not stop. Giggling and remembering, he covered his mouth. His eyes stung, remembering how it was when Billy Boy died of fright.

"Shut up!"

But he could not stop giggling, the same way Billy Boy could not stop bawling that afternoon.

Afterwards Doc Peret had explained: "You see, Billy Boy really died of a heart attack. He was scared he was gonna die—so scared, he had himself a heart attack—and that's what really killed him. I seen it before."

So they wrapped Billy in a plastic poncho, his eyes still wide-open and scared stiff, and they carried him over the meadow to a rice paddy, and then when the Medevac helicopter arrived they carried him through the paddy and put him aboard, and the mortar rounds were falling everywhere, and the helicopter pulled up and Billy Boy came tumbling out, falling slowly and then faster, and the paddy water sprayed up as if Billy Boy had just executed a long and dangerous dive, as if trying to escape Graves Registration, where he would be tagged and sent home under a flag, dead of a heart attack.

"Shut up, for Chrissake!" the soldier hissed, but Paul Berlin could not stop giggling, remembering: scared to death.

Later they waded in after him, probing for Billy Boy with their rifle butts, elegantly and delicately probing for Billy Boy in the stinking paddy, singing—some of them—*Where have you gone, Billy Boy, Billy Boy, Oh, where have you gone, charming Billy?* Then they found him. Green and covered with algae, his eyes still wide-open and scared stiff, dead of a heart attack suffered while—

"Shut up, for Chrissake!" the soldier said loudly, shaking him.

But Private First Class Paul Berlin could not stop. The giggles were caught in his throat, drowning him in his own laughter: scared to death like Billy Boy.

Giggling, lying on his back, he saw the moon move, or the clouds moving across the moon. Wounded in action, dead of fright. A fine war story. He would tell it to his father, how Billy Boy had been scared to death, never letting on . . . . He could not stop.

The soldier smothered him. He tried to fight back, but he was weak from the giggles.

The moon was under the clouds and the column was moving. The soldier helped him up. "You okay now, buddy?"

"Sure."

"What was so bloody funny?"

"Nothing."

"You can get killed, laughing that way."

"I know. I know that."

"You got to stay calm, buddy." The soldier handed him his rifle. "Half the battle, just staying calm. You'll get better at it," he said. "Come on, now."

He turned away and Private First Class Paul Berlin hurried after him. He was still shivering.

He would do better once he reached the sea, he thought, still smiling a little. A funny war story that he would tell to his father, how Billy Boy Watkins was scared to death. A good joke. But even when he smelled salt and heard the sea, he could not stop being afraid.

The 2nd of August 1966

John Gerassi

Matarasso and I spoke to many of the people of Cam Lo that afternoon and evening—to widows and orphans, militia men and peasants, workers and fishermen. But one will forever remain engraved in our memory. She was a pleasant, attractive, thirty-two-year-old worker at the tile factory. Her name was Nguyen Thi Bau. When I met her, she was with her seven-year-old son, Phan Ngoc Bao. Before August 2, 1966, her husband, Phan Ngoc Can, forty-two, had been a district judge. They had four other children: Phan Thi Ngoc Ha, thirteen; Phan Ngoc Huan, eleven; Phan Ngoc Hanh, eight; and Phan Thi Ngoc Hiep, four. Thus, their youngest and oldest were girls.

She began, calmly, softly, obviously under full control:

My husband and I were married on December 23, 1952. We had a very happy marriage. Our oldest girl was thirteen, so we could both work. When we came home in the evening, our kids always received us with joy. They would prepare the meal before we arrived and, over dinner, give us a report on their day's activities. Since I usually got home first, we often walked together part of the way to meet their father. Sometimes, if it was still early, he would take them to the river behind our house for a swim. Our oldest was a good swimmer and the next two were pretty fair. Our children were good students at school; they won many commendations from the teachers. We were a happy family.

We were sitting on some rocks and debris in the area where scores of houses had been demolished. She continued, still outwardly calm, still speaking softly, still quite in control:

And then came the second of August 1966. I went to work at 5 a.m. that day, taking my youngest child, my little four-year-old girl, with me. I had asked my oldest to come to the factory to take her back later. On the way to work, I had bought ten loaves of bread and would ask the oldest to take them back with her. She showed up at the factory at 5.20, but it wasn't time for me to start yet, so we talked for a while. I asked her if papa had left. She said no, that he had a special meeting that day and would go to it directly, so he didn't have to leave home until 6.30. I then told my daughter to hurry home with the bread so he could have some before leaving. She did, and at 5.30 I started my work. I work at the oven where the roof tiles are baked.

A few minutes after I started working I heard the alarm. Like everyone at the factory, I went to the shelter. Then I heard the planes and a lot of explosions. I asked a Militiaman where the bombs had fallen; I knew it must have been fairly near since our shelter was shaken. The Militiaman told me it was in my neighbourhood and told me to rush home. I did, and as soon as I turned the corner over there (pointing), I saw it—our home had vanished.

She rose. We did too. She walked slowly toward a hollowed spot in the ground. 'That's where my house used to be,' she said, still calm, her voice still clear. Then she continued:

Our house had been razed to the ground. But I noticed that my bicycle was at the entrance to the shelter over there. We had built a trench from the house to the garden, so for a second I hoped that everyone in my family had made it. But then I saw my third child, Hanh, being carried on a stretcher. He was dead.

She paused, looked toward the place where the shelter used to be, with Bao at her side walked over to it and, pointing to a small black sign, said: 'That was the shelter.' Still under control, she went on:

A Militiaman was uncovering it. It had been completely buried with dirt from an explosion a few feet away. The first body to be pulled out was my second child Huan, a boy of eleven. The Militiamen who were digging were all our neighbours. I kept calling for help because I knew that the rest of my family must be in the shelter, perhaps still alive though buried with earth. I ran hysterically from side to side until I noticed my youngest son, Bao, this one, all covered with mud and blood but walking, coming toward me. He called 'Mama, Mama.' I found out later that he had been projected out of the shelter and thus, though wounded on his head, cheeks and legs, had survived. I kept hugging him and then took him to the infirmary post so he could be cared for. He was trembling all the time.

She stopped again, sat down. Then, still composed, she continued:

I had hoped and I was still hoping, even then, that the two girls, my oldest and youngest children, had not had time to reach home with the bread and so might still be alive. With great fear, yet hope, I finally pulled myself together and asked Bao as calmly as I could if he had had fresh bread that morning. He said yes. And so I knew my girls had reached home.

While I was at the infirmary, a Militiaman came to tell me that they had found my husband. He was dead. They had also found a neighbour and his four children and another neighbour's child in the same shelter with my husband. Two of the first four were alive, one with a broken skull, the other with a shattered leg. But they were still alive. So, I thought, might be my daughters.

They kept searching for my girls but they couldn't find them. Maybe, I said to myself, Bao was wrong. Or maybe they had gone elsewhere. That night, I was at my husband's funeral when I finally learned that they had found my girls. They were sitting all the way in back of the shelter, my oldest holding my youngest in her arms—buried alive. My youngest child was clutching a piece of bread in her hands.

She got up to go. Where do you live now, I asked her. 'In a room at the factory,' she replied. I asked if I might see it. She hesitated. 'It's very small . . . well, alright.' And we walked together, she with her only surviving child, Matarasso and I, followed by our guides and Haiphong officials, silently, to the factory, down a small alley, to her room. Two beds, one next to the other; a few bits of clothing and a rice-straw rug on the wall. 'I'm sorry it's so dark,' she said, 'but I keep that rug over the window because it gives out on where we were. I don't want to look out there all the time.'

She sat down with Bao on one of the beds and as we talked instinctively reached for a little red book lying on the bed. She fingered it with such feeling that I asked what it was. 'Nothing,' she said, 'just an old diary.' Whose? 'His.' I asked her if there was a passage from it that she wanted to read to us. She hesitated. 'Let's go to the lounge,' she said, and led the way. Once there, she sat down with Bao in an armchair and started reading. Her voice was finally beginning to break:

Every day I try to draw lessons from my work. I try to understand myself, control myself, find what is good and bad in me to develop the former and curtail the latter. I must study myself endlessly. I must learn from the people, learn *with* the people. I must study the books and the history of my work (law). I must learn from friends . . . . I must never take pride in success. I must never despair of failure. I must constantly learn from experience in order to keep progressing.

I asked her if I could have the diary photostated, then, glancing through it I noticed that the last three pages were in a different handwriting. Who wrote this, I asked. Her eyes reddened. 'I did.' May I know what you said? 'The first page, those five lines are just a quick note written after my husband's funeral, on August 2, 1966. The next two pages are a letter to my surviving son, written six weeks later.' Would she read them, I asked. She was reluctant to do so. But she did. Her voice broke completely and tears swelled her eyes, then ran down her cheeks in total abandon. Her first entry was bitter. It read:

I shall never be able to forget that my husband Can and my children Ha, Huan, Hanh and Hiep were killed by the American aggressors. Nor will the hate that I nurture for these assassins ever be extinguished.

The second passage was quite different. It was addressed to the child sitting next to her:

Bao, my dear child. You cannot imagine how much I suffer from the death of your father and brothers and sisters, so much that I have to keep reminding myself that I must go on, that I must endure, in order to bring you up. I must survive for if not, with me dead, you would be all alone, without love. And yet, every day of my life is a Calvary, my darling. Can you ever understand how affected I am by the death of Huan, Hanh, Ha and Hiep? My darling, forgive me, but I would like to die. You are too young to understand, too young to console me. If I could only die, I say to myself, I would no longer suffer. But that would be selfish, and so I shall go on for you and you shall never know how painful it will be for me to live for you.

An hour or so later, Matarasso and I said good-bye to the people of Cam Lo, to our Haiphong hosts, and started the journey back to Hanoi—104 kilometres inland on Route No. 5. It was heavily bombed all the way. 'Well,' said Matarasso, 'at least the centre of Haiphong has not been raided. Did you notice how that city is laid out? Like Venice! Canals everywhere and bridges, so many bridges, and so close to the houses. If your Pentagon decides to go after the bridges, it would be a massacre.'

On April 20, 1967, the United States declared the centre of Haiphong strategic—and began bombing it.

Poems from the West

Latest News
David Craig

They are turning people into hulks of mud.
His hair plastered, clothes messed
To soiled anonymous scraps -
Her shirt and skin and hair
One scab of puddled brown - they stare
At nothing in the world but the point of the knife.

They have abused every common thing -
A knife, water, wire, a jar.
They stick the wire through hands and cheeks -
'You gotta see how quiet dem gooks sit
When we gottem wrapped up like dat.'
They shove them down in the water till they choke,
Throw them out of the helicopters,
Drag them through the paddy tied to a truck.

Unanswered questions, anger at the heat -
These are the latest reasons
For turning a person into a hulk of mud.
Can we sit here any longer
While our own kind choke on swallowed blood?
How can we sleep?

The easiest thing in the world, to eat and sleep -
Our eyelids aren't burnt off, we still have tongues.

It has happened somewhere every year
Since I was young.
I will write about something else
When the torturers have been stopped.
Then it will be natural to study
Or sing an unworried song.

Too Much

They have torn the scalp off every country
They could get their hands on:
The green plumes of Cuba
Scorched off for a coffee crop;
The red soil of Sri Lanka
Bleeding into the sea;
Scotland's glens like scraped wombs
Where nothing will grow again
Except the dark trees of government.
They tore out Ireland's oaks:
"The last furnace was put out in Kerry
When the last wood had been destroyed."
It was the worst thing till Leopold's Congo,
Seven hundred and fifty thousand dead
In eleven years.

Who can graft where they flay?
Who could unburn the seven million Jews?
Who could unplant the Ulster Protestants?

The camps of the refugees in Lebanon
are burning.
The corner pubs in the Falls
Are burning.
The jungle villages in Vietnam
Are burning
In Santiago they are burning the books.

Nobody knows the outcome.
The words of the politicians
Are words.
The wounds have been photographed,
The screams recorded.

Living in this quiet country
We are little better
Than cunning survivors huddled in a cave.

Life at War
Denise Levertov

The disasters numb within us
caught in the chest, rolling
in the brain like pebbles. The feeling
resembles lumps of raw dough

weighing down a child's stomach on baking day.
Or Rilke said it, 'My heart...
Could I say of it, it overflows
with bitterness...but no, as though

its contents were simply balled into
formless lumps, thus
do I carry it about.'
The same war

continues.
We have breathed the grits of it in, all our lives,
our lungs are pocked with it,

the mucous membrane of our dreams
coated with it, the imagination
filmed over with the gray filth of it:
the knowledge that humankind,

delicate man, whose flesh
responds to a caress, whose eyes
are flowers that perceive the stars,

whose music excels the music of birds,
whose laughter matches the laughter of dogs,
whose understanding manifests designs
fairer than the spider's most intricate web

still turns without surprise, with mere regret
to the scheduled breaking open of breasts whose milk
runs out over the entrails of still-alive babies,
transformation of witnessing eyes to pulp-fragments,
implosion of skinned penises into carcass-gulleys.

We are the humans, men who can make;
whose language imagines mercy, lovingkindness;
we have believed one another
the mirrored forms of a God we felt as good —

who do these acts, who convince ourselves
it is necessary; these acts are done
to our own flesh; burned human flesh
is smelling in Viet Nam as I write.

Yes, this is the knowledge that jostles for space
in our bodies along with all we
go on knowing of joy, of love;

our nerve filaments twitch with its presence
day and night,
nothing we say has not the husky phlegm of it in the saying,
nothing we do has the quickness, the sureness,
the deep intelligence living at peace would have

On the War In Vietnam
Goran Sonnevi

Beyond the TV set, outdoors,
the light changed. The dark slowly became
greyish, and the trees looked black
in the clear pale light
of the new snow. Now it is morning,
everything snowed in. I go out
to clear a path.
On the radio I hear the US
has published a white paper
on the VIETNAM war
accusing North Vietnam
of aggression. On TV
last night
we saw a film strip taken with
the Viet-Cong; we could hear
the muffled fluttering
of helicopter propellors
from the ground, from the side being
shot. In another film

a few weeks ago
CBS interviewed American
helicopter pilots. One of them
described how glad he was
when he finally got a shot at
a "V.C.": the rockets
threw the VC about nine feet
straight ahead. There's no doubt
we'll have more snow today,
my neighbor says, dressed in black
on the way to work. He embalms
and is nightwatchman
at an insane asylum. The place where I live - Lund
and outskirts - is becoming a whiter
and whiter paper, the sun rises and lights
the open pages, burning and cold.
The dead are numbers, they lie down, whirl about
like snowflakes, in the country wind. Up till now
they figure 2 million have died in Vietnam.
Here hardly anyone dies
except for personal reasons. The Swedish
economic system doesn't kill
many, at least
not here at home. Here
no one goes to war to protect
his interests. We don't
get burned with napalm
to advance a feudal idea of freedom.
In the 15th and 16th centuries no napalm.
Toward noon here the sun gets rather high.
Soon it will be March 1965.
Every day
more and more dead in America's repulsive war.
There are snowflakes on the photograph
of President Johnson
taken during the last series of bombing raids
on North Vietnam—he is climbing in
or maybe out of a car—more
and more flakes fall on the white pages.
More dead, more self-righteous defenses,
until everything is snowed in again
and the night
finally changes its light outside the windows.

Where is Vietnam
Lawrence Ferlinghetti

Meanwhile back at the Ranch the then President also known
as Colonel Cornpone got out a blank Army draft and began to
fill in the spaces with men and Colonel Cornpone got down to
the bottom of the order where there is a space to indicate just
where the troops are to be sent and Colonel Cornpone got a
faraway look in his eye and reached out and started spinning
a globe of the world and his eye wandered over the spinning
surface of the world and after a long time he said I See No Relief
so they brought him a relief map of the world and he looked
at it a long time and said Thank You Gentlemen I see it all very
clearly now yes indeed everything stands out very clearly now
and I can see the oceans themselves rolling back and Western
Civilization still marching Westward around the world and the
New Frontier now truly knows no boundaries and those there
Vietnamese don't stand a Chinaman's chance in Hell but there's
all these Chinamen who think they do and also think they can
actually reverse the Westward march of civilization and actually
reverse the natural Westward spin of our globe but Gentlemen
these are not War Games this is not Space Angels this is the
real thing Gentlemen and I know right exactly where this here
Vietnam is Gentlemen and I want to make doubly sure that all
our own people know right exactly where this here Vietnam is
Gentlemen in case any of you should happen to get cornered
by some eggheads or someone And just then Ladybird came
running and Colonel Cornpone stepped into the cloakroom and
whispered to her The world really does rotate Westward don't it?
and she being smarter than he as is usually the case whispered
back that this here Vietnam was not a place but a state of mind
and Colonel Cornpone got that old faraway look again and stepped
back onto the front porch and sat there rocking for a long time
and then said Gentlemen I am a family man and this is for real
and I am hereby ordering the complete and final liberation of
Vietmind I mean Vietman for the roots of the trouble are found
wherever the landless and oppressed the poor and despised stand
before the gates of opportunity and are not allowed across the
Frontier into the Great Society which seems to lie out before me
like a land of dreams and so Gentlemen here we go fasten your
seatbelts we are powerful and free and united there ain't much

we can't do and so Gentlemen let me point out to you exactly where it is we all are going on this here globe because Gentlemen even though I am reputed never to have been out of the United States I do know right where we are going on the brink of Vietnam I mean Vietnam and even though we don't want to stop the world spinning in the right direction even for an instant I do want to slow it down just long enough for me to put my finger for you right on this here sore spot which is Vietmine I mean Vietnam and Colonel Cornpone put out his hand to slow down the world just a bit but this world would not be slowed down a bit this world would not stop spinning at all and Texas and Vietnam spun on together faster and faster slipping away under Colonel Cornpone's hand because the surface of this world had suddenly become very very slippery with a strange kind of red liquid that ran on it across all the obscene boundaries and this world went on spinning faster and faster in the same so predestined direction and kept on spinning and spinning and spinning and spinning!

I arrived in Vietnam on my 23rd birthday on 28 March, 1969. I had two reasons for going to Vietnam. I wanted to do something my wife and my mother could be proud of. I wanted to see the United States overrunning North Vietnam.

It was sunny, hot and dry when the men came across that hamlet. It was just another lousy hamlet with eight or ten straw covered huts, only this time the people there made us a bit more angry. They hated the G.I.s, that was quite obvious. When the hundred-odd village people, mostly old men, women and children, had been driven together, the shooting started.

So far as I can remember I had killed three or four. One of the women had a gunshot wound in the neck. It sounded as though she was crying under water. I figure the blood was gushing into her lungs or something. She sank to her knees and fell flat on her face. After the shooting we took three or four ten-year-old girls from the hamlet along with us into the jungle. There were about six of us and they were three or four kids. I suppose each had her turn once or twice. After they had been raped the girls were shot where they were lying. It was a rather nauseating sight.

(Priv. Jerry, 25th Infantry Div.).

Life is plentiful, life is cheap to those people. That is the philosophy of the Orient. You have to realise that an individual life there isn't as important as an individual life in America.

(General Westmoreland).

AFTER A MONTH HERE, WE SHOULD GET A — GOVERNMENT LOAN OF £3,000 TO BUY A HOUSE

AUSTRALIAN SOLDIER IN VIETNAM

My solution? Tell the Vietnamese they've got to draw in their horns and stop aggression or we're going to bomb them back into the Stone Age.

(General Curtis Le May).

Today I got a piece of news that is unbelievable and yet it is true. The enemy has killed her and thrown her body away. She was a guerilla fighter. Pain tears me. I feel half dead. When I was a child I used to love my country for its flowers and butterflies. That's why I got into trouble from time to time for playing truant. Now I love my country because in its earth is the blood and the flesh of my little sister.

(Vietnamese soldier).

Have you ever been involved in an operation during which innocent persons were killed?
We killed anybody we could get hold of.
What about the wounded. Were wounded people killed too?
Yes, they were.
How were they being killed?
With revolvers, rifles, machineguns, or bayonets.
Wounded people lying on the ground? Have you seen such things happen yourself?
I was involved myself.
Why?
After a certain period of time you are like an animal, you do that simply by instinct, you are no longer aware of what is going on.

(Ex-serviceman Richard Dow).

Have you ever been trained to interrogate captured enemies?
Yes, I have.
What were you told about the torture of female captives?
We were told to strip them, place their legs apart and introduce pointed sticks into their vagina. They also said we could rape the girls as often as we wanted to.
Did they also tell you how to use helicopters?
Yes. They found it very amusing to remember that once in Vietnam they had tied the arms and legs of a prisoner to two different helicopters. Then they took off and tore him apart.
Who told you about it?
One of my instructors, a sergeant.
Did he really see that with his own eyes?
He said he had done it.

(Ex-serviceman Chuck Onan).

The CBU 46 cluster bomb unit and the pineapple bomb each contain 250 or 300 steel or plastic pellets which riddle their victims on explosion.

The dum dum bullet, banned under the Hague convention of 1899, was fired from 20-millimetre machine cannon.

The AGM 45 A Shrike projectile explodes into tens of thousands of metal splinters on hitting the ground.

The BLU 25 B Smooth Orange Bomb is a high explosive fragmentation bomb.

The BLU 24 A/A fluted orange bomb ejects 500 sharp-edged particles between 3 and 20 millimetres at high velocity.

The flechette bomb contains tiny barbed nails 3.6 millimetres long.

Incendiary bombs using napalm, thermite, magnesium and phosphorus develop temperatures between 800 and 3,500 degrees centigrade and create sheets of flame saturated with toxic carbon monoxide.

The BLU 82 B Daisy Cutter, weighing 7 tons, has the explosive effect of a small atom bomb destroying all traces of life within a compass of one kilometre.

The cluster bomb unit is a so called mother bomb containing 300 small bombs with thousands of steel or plastic fragments in each.

388,091 tons of napalm bombs were dropped in the Vietnamese war by the United States and its allies between 1963 and 1973. Napalm was also dropped in oil drums from helicopters and fired from flame throwers. In addition, phosphorus, magnesium, and thermite munitions were used. In total, greater quantities of incendiary weapons were used than in any other countries in any other war.

In the decade up to 1971, the U.S. dropped more than one hundred million pounds of herbicides on 5.7 million acres, or more than one seventh of South Vietnam's land area. The chemicals were used to destroy crops and also kill vegetation in areas allegedly occupied by forces of the National Liberation Front. Vietnamese and qualified Western scientists had pointed out that the 'defoliation' program was in reality a program of chemical warfare, causing numerous civilian deaths, especially among the more susceptible infants and elderly. The herbicidal agents used in Vietnam were either forbidden for use in the U.S. or used in dangerous concentration above those permitted by the U.S. Dept. of Agriculture. The gravest long term damage was inflicted on the mangrove forests, which provide charcoal for heating and cooking in the homes of the Vietnamese. Under present conditions of use and natural regrowth, it may take well over 100 years for the mangrove areas to be reforested.

(From a Study sponsored by the Pentagon).

U.S. expenditure on artillery and mortar shells and machine gun and rifle bullets *alone* was 7 million dollars a day.

Throughout the war the explosive equivalent of ten Hiroshima bombs per month was dropped on South Vietnam alone.

A Phantom jet cost 6 million dollars.

An F111 cost 15 million dollars.

A B52 cost 35 million dollars.

An aircraft carrier cost 545 million dollars.

The cost of training a pilot was 500,000 dollars (compared to 50,000 dollars to train a doctor).

More than 8,000 planes were shot down over Indochina.

It was reported in Congress that the cost of killing one guerilla was 400,000 dollars.

The cost of the war rose from 250 million dollars per month in 1966 to over three times that in the seventies.

Let us assume we lose Indochina. The tin and tungsten that we so greatly value from that area would cease coming. So when the U.S. votes 400 million dollars to help that war, we are not voting a give-away program. We are voting for the cheapest way that we can prevent the occurence of something that would be of a most terrible significance to the U.S.A., our security, our power and ability to get certain things we need from the riches of the Indochinese territory and from Southeast Asia.

(president Eisenhower, 1953).

The U.S. never had an ambassador in Vietnam who could say "Hello" in Vietnamese. They never had a decision maker there who spoke Vietnamese. The only one who ever tried was McNamara. He learned how to say "Long live Vietnam!" But when he made his speech at Kennedy Square in Saigon, he got the tones mixed up. He raised his arms in the victory symbol before the 30,000 high school students who had been ordered there to listen and cheer. He began shouting in Vietnamese, not "Long live Vietnam" but "The Southern duck wants to lie down!"

(Don Luce).

There were more than half a million desertions from the U.S. forces between 1965 and 1972. In 1971 alone 79,000 men, the equivalent of six divisions, deserted the army.

(U.S. Office of Manpower & Reserve).

In Boot camp they used to tell us: "Every football team you ever heard of, every athletic team, has lost a game somewhere along the line. The U.S. Military has never lost a war." Well they have now.

(U.S. Soldier).

Give us a nice psychedelic bloodbath and we'll happily reopen all the old wounds. But peace? Hell man, that's a sick thought!"

(U.S. Editor in Saigon).

As we approached the detention hamlets, crowds of kids from the camps began running alongside. The G.I.s were playing a game. They would throw candy out of the windows of their trucks, then swerve to see how close they could come to hitting the kids when they ran for the candy. I saw a kid snaking through the crowd, darting towards the candy, spinning, kneeling, grabbing and rising, prize in hand, facing us, as the edge of the bumper of the truck in front of us caught him in mid-section. He barely had a bruise on him, just a tricked, stunned look on his face. It was the same look I saw on the face of my father as he lay dying in hospital. It was all happening inside. He was dead within 15 minutes. The driver who hit him must have been 19. He kept pacing back and forth saying "I didn't mean it. It didn't happen. I didn't mean it. It didn't happen." The driver of my truck was in a state of near shock. He kept hitting the side of the offending truck with the handle of an entrenching tool. An indignant corporal came up to him. "Hey man, that's the unit's vehicle."

(Jack Kramer).

They saw a woman working in the fields. They shot and wounded her then they kicked her to death and emptied their rifle magazines into her head. They slugged every little kid they came across. Why in God's name does this have to happen?

(Sergeant Gregory Olsen).

There was the noise of course, incredible constant noise. Speading out on the ground was like laying on the back of a truck on the highway, it never stopped vibrating. But what I remember most were the moans. Sometimes the skyhawks would fade and before the B-52s came you could hear acres and acres of moans. That's just what it was like, the moans came in acres. Of course you couldn't see the B-52s when they came. The bombs just came and they turned everything you could see all around us into acres and acres of smoking ash. The moans rose up like smoke, and they were like from some place else, from another world.

(U.S. Soldier).

Ballad of Ho Chi Minh
Ewan MacColl

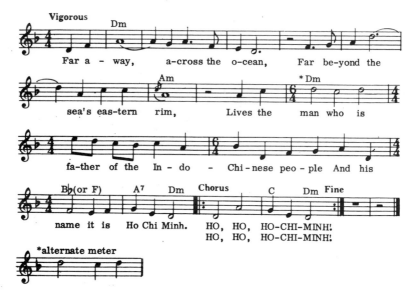

Far a - way, a-cross the o-cean, Far be-yond the sea's eas-tern rim, Lives the man who is fa-ther of the In - do - Chi-nese peo - ple And his name it is Ho Chi Minh.

Chorus

HO, HO, HO-CHI-MINH!
HO, HO, HO-CHI-MINH!

*alternate meter

© Copyright 1967 by STORMKING MUSIC INC.

Far away, across the ocean,
Far beyond the sea's eastern rim,
Lives the man who is father of the Indo Chinese people
And his name is Ho Chi Minh.

CHORUS:

Ho, Ho, Ho Chi Minh!
Ho, Ho, Ho Chi Minh!

From Viet Bac to the Saigon Delta,
From pathless mountains and the plains below,
Young and old, workers, peasants and the toiling tenant farmers
Fight for freedom with Uncle Ho (Chorus)

Ho Chi Minh was a deep sea sailor,
Served his time out on the seven seas;
Work and hardship were part of his early education,
Exploitation his A. B. C. (Chorus)

Ho Chi Minh came home from sailing,
And he looked on his native land,
Saw the want and the hunger of the Indo-Chinese people,
Foreign soldiers on every hand (Chorus)

Ho Chi Minh went to the mountains
And he trained a determined band -
Heroes all sworn to liberate the Indo-Chinese people,
Drive invaders from the land. (Chorus)

Forty men become a hundred,
A hundred thousand, and Ho Chi Minh -
Forged and tempered the army of the Indo-Chinese people,
Freedom's army of Viet Minh. (Chorus)

Every soldier is a farmer,
Comes the evening, and he grabs his hoe;
Comes the morning, he slings his rifle on his shoulder,
This is the army of Uncle Ho. (Chorus)

In the mountains, through the jungles,
In the ricelands and the Plain of Reeds,
March the men and women of the Indo-Chinese army,
Planting freedom with victory's seeds. (Chorus)

From Viet Bac to the Saigon Delta,
March the armies of Viet Minh -
And the wind stirs the banners of the Indo-Chinese people,
"Peace" and "Freedom" and Ho Chi Minh! (Chorus)

The Fields of Vietnam

Freely

1. O broth-ers, though we're stran-gers and your land_____ and mine are far a-part, And though your name lies awk-ward-ly and strange_____ up-on my tongue, As the nee-dle's drawn to-wards the pole, So I am drawn both heart and soul To_____ sing of your great strug-gle in the fields of Vi-et-nam.

© Copyright 1967 by STORMKING MUSIC INC.

O, brothers, though we're strangers and your land and mine
   are far apart,
And though your name lies awkwardly and strange upon my
   tongue,
As the needle's drawn towards the pole,
So I am drawn both heart and soul—
To sing of your great struggle in the fields of Viet Nam.

Your barefoot farmers would not wear the yoke and chains
   of slavery—
For four long bitter years they fought the armies of Japan;
Your flesh opposed their armoured might
You harried them by day and night—
And you drove them from the jungles and fields of Viet Nam.

Before you could draw peaceful breath more death was raining
   from the skies,
The French came, and for nine more years your land they overran;
But the enemy could not subdue,
They broke at Dien Bien Phu—
And their dead lay all around them in the fields of Viet Nam.

The French had scarcely left your shores when more invading
   armies came,
Equipped with all the latest tools men use to kill a man;
"We've come to show you," was their cry,
"All the ways a man can die—
And we'll make a bloody desert of the fields of Viet Nam."

The skies by day were dark with planes, with hungry flames
   the nights were red.
The stench of death lay on the air with reek of spent napalm;
Death bloomed in every paddy field,
And still your people would not yield—
To American invaders in the fields of Viet Nam.

For thirteen years the U.S. Army's sown your soil with
   blood and tears,
Impartially they deal out death to woman, child and man,
And still no victory—instead
They count their own dishonoured dead,
And contempt's their only harvest in the fields of Viet Nam.

O, brothers, where did you find strength to fight so long for
   freedom's cause?

A quarter-century has passed since first your fight began;
Long have you fought, and valiantly,
And so long as men love liberty—

They will sing of your great struggle in the fields of Viet Nam.

Oh, Brother, Did You Weep

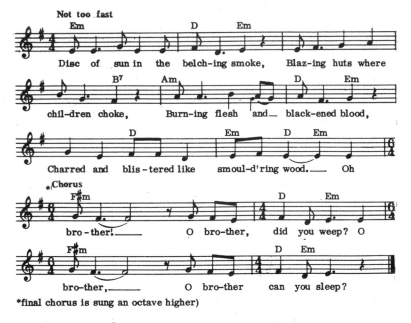

Not too fast

Disc of sun in the belch-ing smoke, Blaz-ing huts where chil-dren choke, Burn-ing flesh and black-ened blood, Charred and blis-tered like smoul-d'ring wood. Oh bro-ther! O bro-ther, did you weep? O bro-ther, O bro-ther can you sleep?

*Chorus

*final chorus is sung an octave higher)

© Copyright 1967 by STORMKING MUSIC

Disc of sun in the belching smoke,
Blazing huts where children choke,
Burning flesh and blackened blood,
Charred and blistered like smould'ring wood.

CHORUS:
Oh brother! Oh brother, did you weep?
Oh brother! Oh brother, can you sleep?

Wall-eyed moon in the wounded night,
Touching poisoned fields with blight,
Showing a ditch where a dead girl lies:
Courted by ants and hungry flies. (Chorus)

Scream of pain on the morning breeze,
Thunder of bombs in the grove of trees,
Hymn of rubble and powdered stone
Anguished flesh and splintered bone. (Chorus)

Programmed war, efficiency team,
Punch cards fed to thinking machines,
Computor death and the murder plan:
Total destruction of Vietnam.

LAST CHORUS:
O brother, have you got no shame?
O Jesus! They're killing in my name.

The Village in the Forest
Nguyen Trung Thanh

The village is within firing range of the enemy post. They are in the habit of opening fire twice in the day. In mid-morning and at evening, or at noon and again at nightfall, sometimes about midnight and again at first cock-crow. Practically all their shells fall among the trees by the side of the great river. In this forest, which is thick with hundreds and thousands of the tree we call Xa-nu, not one has been spared. Many are half broken and swing and crack when there is a storm; from their wounds the resinous sap springs, filling the whole region with an unforgettable aromatic scent. Oozing and glittering in the strong light of summer, it quickly becomes a dark sticky mass, very much like a great clot of blood.

But beside every Xa-nu that falls there are already four or five young saplings springing up, pointing to the sky. Xa-nu is a remarkably quick growing tree. The very young growth that has been ploughed up by the shells dies after five or six days, but the shells can do no harm to saplings that have passed the height of a man and whose foliage is already strong and tufty, they are like birds that are fully fledged. Wounds heal quickly in a healthy and vigorous body and these grow rapidly to replace the ones that are fallen.

So it has happened during these recent years that the forest of Xa-nu has become thicker than ever, as though it were making a special effort to shelter the village.

After three years in the Liberation forces, Thu has managed to arrange a visit to his native village. Little Heng who met up with him by the river serves as guide.

When Thu left his home Heng was no higher than his belt, he had not even learnt how to run about gathering and selling firewood, but dressed in a diminutive loin cloth he used to follow the workers to the furrowed fields. And now here he is, full of pride in his long gun, taking on the responsible job of guide.

It is the same old path through the plantations of manioc and banana which always in old days led to his home village. The way is rugged, cut in terraces, serpentined under and around the thickets of broom, swarming with leeches in the rainy season.

Thu knows every inch of the way home, but for nothing in the world would he venture the path alone without a guide, the way is stuffed with snares and booby traps. Over all this area, well hidden, there are countless arrows ready to pierce, boulders ready to crush, spikes ready to cut the intruder to pieces without mercy.

Heng who has grown up too suddenly is as sparing of words as the rest of the inhabitants of his village of Xo-Man. Wearing a cap given him by a soldier of the Liberation Army and a shirt which hangs down to his knees, quite covering his loin cloth, he nevertheless carries a full sized gun in a bandolier like a true soldier. From time to time, as they reach tricky places in their journey he turns his face up to Thu with a sly smile as though to inquire, "What about this, Big Brother?" His eyes shine suddenly with an alert sparkle and there is an air of undisguised pride in his bearing; Thu grins back, wagging his head approvingly.

When they came to a little spring by the wayside which bubbles out of a bamboo pipe stuck into the rock Heng calls a halt. "You may wash your feet here but not drink. Our sister Dzit will scold you if you drink cold water when you are too hot." Thu smiles, "Dzit is medical superintendent?" "Oh no. Sister Dzit is party secretary of our branch and she is also political adviser to the village armed forces." "I see." Thu obediently refrains from drinking. Instead he removes his cap, opens his shirt, leans forward and splashes the water all over his head and face. The icy coolness of the water is a delicious shock and the blood beats vigorously in his temples. He is thinking, "So . . . . Dzit has become Party Secretary!" but he finds it quite impossible to imagine her as she must be now. At the time of her sister Mai's death when he left the village she had been no more than a little girl, naked to the waist. During the cold nights, he remembers, she didn't sleep but stayed close to the fire until dawn to be ready to go and beat rice in the place of her dead sister. Conscientiously she beat and filled the thirty measures for the bag that Thu was to take with him.

Always solemn, saying nothing, her eyes remained dry though everyone else, even old grandpapa Met, could weep for the loss of Mai.

Heng is determined to take good care of Thu. "You will catch a fever splashing so long in freezing cold water. Come on, let's move. It's getting late." Cap in hand Thu obediently follows in the footsteps of his young guide.

At the verge of the thickets of broom a great tree lies across the path along the side of which the guerillas have dug a trench. There is a bit of climbing to be done. Thu pauses for a moment remembering that when he went away the great tree was still standing. Here it was, just here, that he met Mai for the first time. Not really the first time, of course. Children of the same village, they had known each other since they were carried on their mothers' backs.

But it was here that he found her for the first time after his escape from prison. Here he saw how she had grown up. She had cried as she held him by his two hands — in those days still unmutilated. She wept not any more as a child cries, they were the warm tears of a young girl in whom a kind of reluctance is struggling with a new and uncontrollable tenderness. This memory pierces his entrails suddenly like a spear of sharpened bamboo.

Little Heng knows nothing of all this. Having climbed up on to the tree trunk he turns back with an impatient toss of the head. "Hey, brother Thu, come on! You've been away a long time. Have you forgotten how to climb?"

Thu clears the tree trunk, the path that descends from this point is stuffed with snares and trip-wires. Frowning with concentration Thu follows his guide in silence until suddenly he catches the familiar sound of his village, the perpetual pounding of pestles in the grain mortars. It seems to him that this familiar sound is what he has missed the most when he has thought with longing of his native village during the course of these three years of absence. Since before he was weaned he heard these sounds of the incessant work of the women of his people, the Stra, a national minority in Vietnam; work in which his mother, Mai and Dzit also had their share in times gone by.

He has to make an effort to keep calm for his heart is beating like a drum. He keeps knocking his feet against tree roots as the path begins its descent into the village. He starts running in front of Heng, Heng shouting after him, "Look out for the traps! It isn't safe any more to run like that. Stop! Don't go in front!" When at last they arrive the sun has not quite left the sky. Throwing his gun down Heng shouts at the top of his voice, "Hey everyone, Hey good people, here is a visitor!" From the door of every house pop four or five startled faces, all eyes round with surprise, then follows a chorus of exclamations, "Oh Heavens! Oh God's mercy — it's Thu — he's here!" "Is that really the one and only Thu?" Some cannot even spare the time to descend the bamboo ladder but jump straight from the house platform to the ground. Old bent grandmothers descend cautiously step by step swearing, "Oh what a lad! This is an occasion. You might have waited till my funeral to make a party of it!" The young girls hold back from the general rush, modestly remaining indoors, hiding, peeping and chattering.

The village forms a circle round Thu and Thu takes pains to recognise everybody. Here is Grandpa Tang still wearing his beard in a kind of ruff with the additional feature of a fine long stemmed pipe made out of a piece of metal from a shot-down American helicopter. Here is brother Pro who has grown old, sister Blom with hair that is turning grey, the good old Phoi with not a single tooth in his head. A rabble of little children with their faces fantastically smeared with the soot of Xa-nu wood fires. But where is Grandpa Met? Thu is on the point of asking when a hand like a vice grips his shoulder, he turns and there is Met himself. The old man is still as solid and full of vitality as ever, his beard still black and lustrous now reaches to the middle of his chest, his eyes are the same, oblique and sparkling, the scar on his right cheek still seems to glitter. He is naked to the waist, showing a full round chest like the trunk of a great Xa-nu tree. The grandfather pushes off Thu to have a proper look at him from head to foot, then he bursts into a roar of characteristic laughter. "Ha ha! Here you are and with a Tommy gun! Well, soldier of the Army of Liberation — everything's fine, eh!" Thu well knows the old man, he never gratifies anybody with a "Well done!" or anything like "Welcome home, hero!" When you can see that he is most pleased all he can say is "everything's fine!"

When Grandpa Met speaks everyone listens. His words have authority. Although nearing sixty his voice is still sonorous and vibrates powerfully in his great chest. "Well, how many nights are they allowing you? Only one? — but that's O.K. If it's one night's leave you stay one night. If you have two nights you stay two. Orders are orders. Tonight you stay with me." No-one raises an objection. He continues, "Now let's all go in again. The day is ended. We can make our fires and have supper. You kids clean yourselves up a bit — no more smuts, eh! You don't need to paint yourselves up any more like play-actors. If you don't wash it all off properly I shall have something to say — you hear? Thu my son, you'll need to wash your feet. You'll not have forgotten where our fountain is? Good, that's fine! If you could ever forget we'd have to chase you out to hide in the woods." Already Grandpa Met has taken charge of the Tommy gun and the haversack and himself conducts Thu to the fountain at the end of the village. The children joyously escort them.

At the fountain several young girls, whose faces Thu seems to know without being able to attach names to them, are filling their long bamboo water-carriers. They scatter hastily to leave the well to him. He has already washed at the stream, but there is no harm in washing again. Having removed his shirt he lets the jet of cold water play over his head, his back and his chest, leaning over the familiar stone basin a corner of which is permanently indented where old Met is in the habit of sharpening his machete.

The Grandfather contemplates in silence the broad back of the young man. The old wounds are marked there very clearly still, dark scars striped all over the back. As he looks tears come which he furtively wipes away. Thu is too much occupied to notice. Only the children have seen and are amazed.

From the roofs of the houses thin threads of smoke are rising into the evening shadows.

On this festive evening at the house of Grandpa Met the rather insipid arrowroot soup is followed by the special dish of fish in sour sauce which Met reserves for the entertainment of guests who have come from far. Thu takes out his travelling rations and offers a tin of salt. "We have half a gallon left," says Met, "a favour allotted to Dzit by the district authorities at the time of the Festival of Chosen Fighters. Dzit divided it among all the families. The portion that remains is reserved for the sick. Yes, I think we will try your salt." The old man does not put the precious salt in the soup, he hands out a few grains to each person, everyone tastes it, carefully holding it a long time on the tongue the better to enjoy its savour.

The white rice is mixed with a good deal of tapioca; lifting the bowl the Grandfather explains, "This year there was no famine in the village, the rice lasted from one harvest to the next. But each household agreed to economise to try to reserve enough for three years." Then suddenly he asks, "Your fingers, Thu . . . . they are still stumps? They don't grow again, eh?" He lowers the bowl from his lips to continue in a voice tight with anger, "But in our village how many are acquainted with that tale? Never mind, even if the fingers have but two joints left they remember all right how to pull a trigger . . . . tell me, did you come through the forest by the riverside? The Xa-nu is still flourishing there. If a tree falls there, a young one springs up in its place. I defy them to destroy that forest . . . . but come on, eat your rice. Our rice, the white rice of the Stra people, is better than any other, my boy!"

At the conclusion of the feast somebody in the communal village house sounds a rattle, making three distinct separate flourishes at the end. This is the signal that everyone in the village is invited to assemble in the house of Met. The young girls extinguish their torches at the top of the ladder before coming in. The old women, on the other hand, bring their torches right up to have a good look at Thu. They look at him long and searchingly, then throw their brands in the hearth where they flame and crackle. An old man climbing the ladder shouts for all to hear, "Where's our lad Thu — have you fed him properly, Met?" The voice of an old woman is heard inside, "Now then, you men, make a bit of room for Dzit. Here, Dzit, my honey, come and sit here." Thu raises his head to look for Dzit and sees her already seated, her legs folded to one side while with one hand she is pulling at her skirt till it covers her heels.

Suddenly Thu experiences a pang of recognition. It is quite incredible that Dzit, grown up, could look so exactly like her

136

sister. The stumpy nose of Dzit has developed straight and fine, well marked eyebrows over clear calm eyes.

Dzit too takes a very long look at Thu, then in a voice of studied detachment — "Comrade, your permit of entry, please." "What permit?" Thu says uncomprehendingly. "The permit from the authorities — for you to come home. Without your papers you are not allowed in and the Committee will have to put you under arrest." Thu gives a shout of laughter. He is on the point of replying that having an unbearable fit of homesickness he has simply run off for the day, but under the severe gaze of Dzit he takes out of his pocket a small slip of paper which he gives her. "Comrade responsible for the political instruction of the armed forces of the community, I am at your service." Dzit takes the paper, studies it by the light of the fire. A dozen heads turn round, some little ones try to spell out the characters. For a long moment Dzit looks at the paper. She is reading it over to herself several times. "Is it in order?" asks Grandpa Met. Dzit hands back the paper to Thu with a smile. "It is in order. But why only one night?" She herself supplies the answer. "Anyway that's fine. One night is enough for the village to see you again for a while." She pauses. "We think about you often." Laughter, jokes and inquiries, suspended for a while, start up again louder than ever, filling the house. The ringing voice of Old Met can be heard through all the others. "Ah well, that's O.K.!" He shoves away one or two small boys and comes to sit beside his visitor near the fireplace. He thumps the bowl of his pipe on the hob in the hearth, breaks off a splinter of bamboo from the screen and with elaborate care proceeds to scrape round the pipe's interior to remove the dottle clean and whole. At last he raises his head and looks around him. Everyone is now waiting in silence. Grandpa Met is about to tell the story of the evening. Outside the rain falls gently with a murmur that is indistinguishable from the sighing of the wind in many leaves. The Grandfather has no need to raise his voice from its deep and sonorous rumble. "All the old ones here know the story. Among the young there are those who know it and some who do not." He looks significantly at the smallest ones, who, appreciating the grave tones of his words, are already all ears. "Our brother Thu has at last come home," he continues with one hand resting on the shoulder of the young fighter. "Our brother Thu whose story I have told so many times is here among us again, come from the Liberation Army which is fighting for our freedom. This day he has come back to see his home village. His Commander has granted him one night's leave, his signature is on the paper which our Party Secretary has just read. He is one of us. A Stra. His parents died young. It was the village that reared him. His boyhood was hard but his heart is as clear as the spring that waters our village of Xo-Man. Tonight I will tell again his story to give him a proper welcome. Listen well, Stra people. All who have ears, all who have a heart that loves our mountain land, loves our country. Listen well and remember, so that when I am no longer here to tell stories you can make it your duty to pass on this piece of our history to our descendants.''

Everyone remains silent. So quiet that the splashing of the distant waterfall can clearly be heard mingled with the multitudinous sigh of rain on the forest leaves.

Thu looks at Grandpa Met. The wavering flicker of the fire lights up the bulk of the patriarch, who seems like one of those figures from history whose deeds were sung in long ballads that Thu remembers from childhood. Then his glance moves to Dzit. She reminds him of Mai as she was when they met at the edge of the wood. Dzit also sits listening now with calm and thoughtful eyes.

"The old ones have forgotten nothing, only the dead have forgotten, but they have left their memory with the living. At the time I am telling you about the Diêm government mercenaries occupied all this region, all the great mountain and forest lands. They ravaged around in our forests like wild pig. The soldiers carried bayonets red with blood — as red as their berets. Thu still quite young stood no higher than my belt, but he was as nippy as a squirrel. The old have not forgotten, and there are many quite young who remember, Thu as he was then hardly as high as the belt of Old Met. Thu has not forgotten how he carried a bag that had been his mother's. In it there were a few vegetables — these were on top, but underneath, well hidden, were two bowls of good white rice. He dodged like a little animal in and out the steep rock crevices, he ran on his short legs all through the forest ways to take food to the guerilla cadres hiding in the jungle. A little girl even smaller than himself struggled along after him. She tucked up the frock, that her mother had made for her, to jump from rock to rock. Like a little finch she hopped, twittering all the time and calling after him in a plaintive pipe, 'Thu, Thu wait, please wait for me!' And Thu would turn round, his eyes all indignant. 'Whisht, Mai, you squeak like a bloody one-eyed magpie!' Mai would have laughed but didn't dare.

"The revolutionary cadre hiding at this time in the forest was called Quyet. Since the mercenaries had occupied our mountains and forests not a day passed without a raid on some village, not a night but we could hear their guns and their dogs roaring and howling through the forest. Nevertheless, our village people took pride in the fact that in five years of oppression not a single resistance fighter had been caught or killed in all our mountain region.

"At first it was the young men who brought food to the guerillas and kept watch for them. Then the soldiers got wind of this. They arrested the young men and they hanged our brother Xut from a branch of the fig tree that grows at the entrance to our village. 'A warning,' they announced, 'to those who feed Communists.' They followed this up by forbidding the young men to go to work in the forests. So it was the old ones after that who took over the job from the young. The guerillas and the Revolutionary Cadres continued to be fed and guarded, till again the enemy discovered what was going on. They killed mother Nhan and exhibited her severed head, tied by the hair to the barrel of a gun. Finally the children had to replace the old ones. Among our little ones the bravest were Thu and Mai. If Thu went to work in the fallow land it was Mai who wandered off to visit the guerilla. When Mai stayed at home to mind her little sister Dzit it was Thu who went to the hideout in the forest.

"Often they went together. It was not right that the Party Cadre should be left unguarded. If the enemy should find where he was hiding and start a chase who would serve as his guide in the unknown forest? Quyet asked them one day, 'My little friends, are you not afraid of being captured by the enemy? They will kill you as they killed brother Xut and mama Nhan.' Thu, who was just curling himself up in the arms of Quyet, jumped up. Grandpa Met said, 'The Revolutionary guerilla represents the Resistance, and as long as the Resistance is here, the mountains and the forests and the springs are ours.'

"In the forest Quyet began to teach Thu and Mai to read. He split bamboos into laths which he stuck together to make writing boards as big as three handspans. Then the three confederates made a blackboard which they blackened with the soot of Xa-nu, then coated the surface with the thick resin, proof against all scrubbing. Then Thu made a three days' trek all the way to Mount Ngoc Linh to find white stones which he brought back in his bag to serve as chalk for the teacher.

"Mai, more nimble-minded than Thu, learnt to read in three months, then to write. After six months she could calculate figures. Thu was slower and easily lost patience. Having arrived at the letter "Y" he had already forgotten that the letter "O" finished with a tail made Q. One day, in front of Mai and Quyet he smashed the bamboo writing board to bits and went off to sulk beside the river. Quyet went to comfort him but Thu would not speak. When Mai went to him he wanted to hit her. So Mai just sat down beside him. 'If you aren't going back to school neither shall I. I am not going without you . . . . Come, brother, I've made another writing board for you.' At this Thu picked up a stone and struck it hard against his own head till the blood ran down.

Quyet had to bandage it. That night in the cave where they all slept, putting his arms round Thu, Quyet said to him softly, 'Have you ever thought that if they kill me, the one to replace me as Party Cadre will be you? How will you become a good leader if you don't study and go on studying?' Thu, pretending to be asleep, surreptitiously wiped his tears. The next morning he called Mai to him, 'Mai, will you tell me how they say that letter that looks like "O" but with a sort of tail, and that letter with the big belly.' Mai wrote the letter with the big belly on the new board that she had made for him. She spoke softly, 'It is the letter "B", 'Yes, of course, its "B", what a fool I am!'

"If Thu found it easy to forget his letters he was amazing when it came to scrambling about the mountains. He acted as liaison for Comrade Quyet and from the local Commune to the district committee. He never took a route where there was evidence of feet having passed that way before. When the enemy appeared to be closing in from every direction he would climb up the highest tree to take in the general pattern of their movements, then cut directly across their lines, avoiding the danger of encirclement. Crossing rivers he would choose the most wild and rapid reach and swim it, slicing under the surface or leaping through the waves like a young otter. He reckoned the mercenaries from the towns would be likely to look for the partisans where the water flowed evenly. 'They wouldn't be likely to look for us where it's rough.'

"But there came a time as he was shooting a rapid in the river Dac Nang with a letter from Comrade Quyet for the district committee (well rolled up in a green leaf hidden in his mouth) when a rifle bullet grazed his ear. Thu was just able to swallow the message. He found himself in an ambush.

"Three days later the people of Xo-man saw an enemy detachment bringing little Thu into the village, heavily bound. 'Point out the Communists if you don't want to die!' The usual thing . . . . all the village gathered round the child. Old Met was at his side and the boy still stood no higher than his belt. The Grandfather said to him in our own tongue in a voice grave and low, 'Thu, you will not dishonour our village.' Thu replied with his eyes. No mistake. 'That's fine,' says the old man. The boy's back was gashed with knife wounds. 'Where are the Communists? Show them!' Thu said in a low voice, 'Untie me then, if you want me to point for you.' They freed one arm. With the freed hand Thu pointed to his belly. 'There's one.' Another slash with the knife. From his back, no bigger than the bag he used to carry, the dark blood sprang. Before the end of that day it was to become black and sticky like the resin of Xa-nu. When they led Thu away, Mai rushed to him crying bitterly.

He said, 'Don't cry. Study hard. If they kill me you must do my job.'

"Three years later Thu succeeded in making his escape from the prison of Kontum. The wounds in his back had healed. When he reached the great tree on the edge of the broom thickets on his way home it was Mai who was waiting for him and she took his hands in hers. He was amazed to see how she had grown up. That night all the village came to the house of Old Met exactly as on this night."

The voice of Old Met resounded like an echo from that unforgotten night. "It was exactly then as now. This same hearth and the fire and the rain streaming on and on. I was sitting here, Thu there with Mai beside him as Dzit is now — you remember, Thu? Yes, my dears, it is the same. Rain in the big leaves of the fig tree outside, the fire of Xa-nu always gently glowing away and everyone in the village united together to welcome our brother who had got himself out of the prison of Kontum. Mai was sitting there looking at Thu with the same black eyes shining under her dark brows — just like Dzit, perhaps a little less grave and a little more devoted but just as calm, just as resolute as our sister Dzit. But at that time Old Met was not in the habit of telling stories as he does now, he simply announced, 'Thu, Mai has a letter for you from Comrade Quyet, if you would read it out then everyone could listen.' I must explain that some time after the arrest of Thu Comrade Quyet was called away for regrouping to Seventh Regional Headquarters. It happened that on the way he was seriously wounded in an ambush and died soon after. Before he died he dictated this letter to our village. Thu took the paper and read it by the light of the fire.

"Comrades Thu, Mai, and my brothers of Xo-man,' it said, 'I am dying. You who remain must prepare spears, lances, javelins, crossbows and arrows, shields, cleavers, every kind of weapon. You must hide them in the forest where it is impossible for the enemy to discover them. The day will come for them to be used. As for Thu, he must go on with his studies in order to take my place as Party Organiser.'

"When Thu had read the letter the whole village rose up and followed Old Met out into the rain which fell heavier as the night advanced. They went into the depths of the forest to find their weapons, spears, arrows, javelins, shields and bows, that they had made and kept hidden. Later Thu made a three-day expedition to Mount Ngoc Linh, not this time to fetch a bag of white stones, but to load himself up with whet-stones, for on the summit of Ngoc Linh there is a quarry of these sufficient to supply at least a hundred simultaneous armed insurrections. Then night after night the village of Xo-Man sharpened its weapons in the dark hours. During the day they followed Old Met into the jungle to clear the undergrowth for the planting of cassava trees for food; these soon sprang up all around and grew well.

"But somehow a rumour that the village of Xo-Man was preparing weapons got to the ears of the enemy at the post of Dac Ha. It was the season of the rice harvest, not long after the birth of the first child of Mai and Thu. An enemy detachment suddenly appeared in the village. The commander of this detachment was Dzuc, as it happened the same commander who had raided us before when Thu was taken.

"He wore a beret as red as blood and he roared out for all to hear, 'Thu again — by God — this is his doing! So the tiger was not sufficiently beaten! Here he is again stirring up trouble all over the place.'

"Meanwhile Thu and Met were busy hiding the young all round the village in the trees and rocks and caves near at hand. The enemy remained four nights in our midst. The fury of their whips spared none. Cries and screams could be heard all the time. Dzuc, with his revolver constantly in hand, threatened the people, 'All those found outside the village will be shot without mercy — on the spot!' No-one dared leave the village except Dzit; tiny and agile, she slithered at dusk along the bamboo water conduit to bring food to those in hiding outside the village.

"Early in the morning of the fourth day an enemy guard grabbed the little girl as she came in from the forest. They took the poor child into the middle of the village place, loaded a tommy gun, then slowly fired a series of near misses all round her. The shots whistled past the child's ears, singed her hair, and ploughed up the dust around her feet, her skirt was torn to shreds. At every shot she screamed until at the tenth shot, suddenly the tears dried up and there were no more cries. After that her body shuddered like a spring at each succeeding shot but her eyes were seen to fix the torturers with a strange calm, the same mature calm you see today in the eyes of our Party Secretary.

"Having failed with the little girl, Dzuc tried another, more effective trick. 'When one holds the tigress and the cub, the tiger will soon appear!'

"He ordered the arrest of Mai.

"Thu who was hidden in a tree beside the village fountain overheard these words. From his place of concealment it is possible to see very clearly what is going on in the village place. The hand of Thu savagely clutched the trunk of that tree when he saw the brutes leading Mai to the middle of the place. On her back she had her little child, only a month old.

"Dzuc proceeded with the questioning. 'Where is your husband, dirty Communist?' Mai who had just been given a blow on the side readjusted her precious burden and raised her eyes to look in the face of Dzuc.

" 'So you can't speak, you bitch!' Then he turned to swear at his men, 'Why are you standing there like dummies!'

"A large fat soldier casting a twisted look at Dzuc took a long steel rod and sidled up to Mai. He stuck out his tongue to lick his lips then slowly raised the metal bar. Mai cried out at this, fiercely undoing the knotted cloth in which her baby was slung, she had barely time to bring it round under her breast before the rod came down with force upon her back.

" 'Well, where is Thu?'

"The steel bar this time caught her on the side just as the mother moved the baby back on to her shoulders. Again she was struck on the back with the child caught against her heart. The blows quickened. The cries of the mother were no longer heard. Suddenly a piercing scream was torn from the child. It is quickly finished . . . . nothing more but the sound of the iron rod pounding a human pulp.

"Thu sprang from his hiding place in the fig tree. His hand was full of crushed fruit and leaves. He rushed in among the soldiers. He lost consciousness of what he did. The huge soldier was stretched flat in the middle of the village place and Dzuc took to his heels as though the Devil was after him. All round sounded the click of safety catches. He clutched Mai and the dead child. But he could not save Mai.

"Thu was not able to save Mai and her child from death." The voice of old Met sounds hoarse. He clumsily rubs a tear from his eye, then continues in a firmer voice, "No, he couldn't save his wife and child. Mai died that night. The child was already dead. A blow from the fat soldier's rod had killed it before the mother, falling to the ground, could save it with her body. You remember Thu? You couldn't save your wife. You hands were *empty,* so they were able to overpower you. As for me, I remained hidden in the fig tree. I saw them tie you up with lianas. I did not throw myself away to save you, for I too had empty hands. I stayed hidden and then went into the forest. I went back to look for the young ones hiding there. They had gone to fetch our sharpened weapons. Have you heard well, my children? Have you heard well? Remember what I have told you. When I shall no longer be in this world, you who live on, it will be your duty to tell it all to the coming generations. The enemy came with guns . . . . As for us, as I told you, we could only arm ourselves with spears and javelins.

"They tied Thu up with lianas and dragged him to the village communal house where they threw him into a corner. Then they went to stuff their guts on pig flesh stolen from the village.

"Thu lay there in a corner while the light thickened to dusk. He was astonished to find himself so calm. The child was dead. Mai also must have died. 'I shall die too,' he thought. 'Who will be Party Cadre after me? When the time comes for the Party to give the order to rise and fight who will be the one to lead the comrades of Xo-Man in the struggle? Grandpa Met is too old. Soon Dzit will be old enough, and that girl will be as steadfast as her sister — perhaps even tougher. It'll be all right, only it's a pity I can't live to see the day when our village takes arms against tyranny.'

"Meanwhile Dzuc had a huge fire made in the hearth of the communal house and ordered all the people to stand round. Having cut Thu's bonds he barked out to the people of the village, 'We have information that you have been making weapons. Those who have been guilty may now watch the hands of Thu.'

"With a jerk of his chin he signed to the gross soldier who took from his cartridge belt a bunch of rags. With these rags soaked in the resin of Xa-nu he tied up each of Thu's ten fingers. He then picked up a burning stick, but at this point Dzuc stepped forward. 'My job!' he said, grabbed the stick, and began to laugh. He waved the burning stick in Thu's face. 'Now we're going to have a good look down the throat of this red menace who plans to take arms against us. You pathetic creatures, you weren't born to carry spears and javelins. This lesson is for you — mark it well and give up your stupid notions.'

"One finger burst into flame then another and another as the fire touched them. Nothing catches fire more quickly than the resin of Xa-nu. The fire sprang instantly and the ten fingers of Thu became ten torches. Thu shut his eyes, then opened them again and kept them open, looking firmly before him. His teeth tore his lips, blood filled his mouth, but he never cried out. Had not comrade Quyet said, 'A Communist never flinches, never sues for mercy?'

"Dzuc went on laughing, laughing hysterically. But suddenly a great uproar began, feet running all round the house. Thu then let himself cry, a single cry which merged into a general shout of voices coming in on all sides, and a great storm of stamping feet, thundering nearer, overwhelming the smothered cries of the soldiers. Then the voice of Old Met rang out with the order, 'Cut them up, boys!'

"He was there, Grandpa Met, standing with a long javelin in his right hand and Dzuc grovelling on the ground under its point. And the young ones, all the lads of the village were there, each one with a spear glittering in the firelight, sharpened on the stones that Thu had fetched from Mount Ngoc Linh.

"The voice of our elder brother Broi was heard, solemn and

calm. 'Thu, Thu. Hold up your head! We have won. Look up. The people have beaten the enemy with spears and javelins!'

"The fire had left the fingers of Thu but it still burnt red in the midst of the house. The bodies of the soldiers were heaped about the burning embers. Old Met rested his lance on the floor and shouted out for all to hear. 'So, it has begun! Now let us light the signal fires. Let everyone, the old as well as the young, women and men, arm themselves with spears and javelins. Let those who have none take sharpened bamboo staves. Come on, let's light the fires!'

"Gongs were sounded, all the gongs of the village of Xo-Man. From the wooded plateau where the Xa-nu trees grow beside the river, all night long a great agitation and stirring could be heard. Fires sprang out of the thickets all round, shining out into the night."

Not one of the listeners has noticed that the night is already far gone. The rain has been falling for some time in heavier drops. Old Met raises his head, looks round at everyone. The beard that covers his chest quivers as he says finally, "There, that's the end of my story. From that night the village went to war. Thu also went when his fingers were healed. The wounds scarred over but the top joint of each finger was missing. But it is possible to throw a javelin or press a trigger with what is left. Thu went off to take his part in the Revolution.

"On the far side of the mountain Ngoc Linh there was a village which suffered under the scourge of another Dzuc, they too had taken up arms. It was this village that called for Thu's help. He went and has not returned to us till this very evening."

Thu stands up, stretches his limbs, moves towards the hearth where he remains motionless for a while. From the enemy post the cannon never ceases to pound away at the forest of Xa-nu beside the great river. But no-one takes any notice. Memories of the past have obliterated its distant thunder.

And now it is time for Thu to go back to his unit. Old Met and Dzit accompany him as far as the forest beside the river.

The firing of the previous night has felled several of the big trees. The resin that has oozed from their wounds has dried and glistens in the rays of the summer sun. All around innumerable saplings have sprung from the earth. There are some which have scarcely pierced the ground but already the little thrusting points are drawn upward like tiny bayonets.

The three stand there gazing into the distance. Nothing is to be seen but the great forests of Xa-nu stretching to the remote horizon.

(Translated by Mary Cowan).

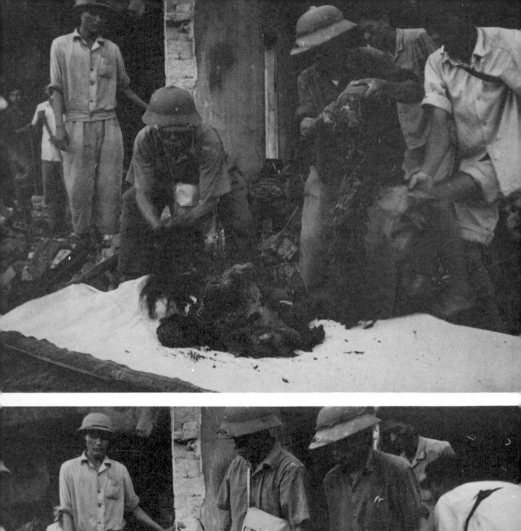

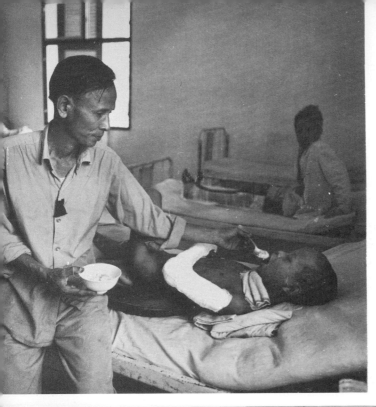

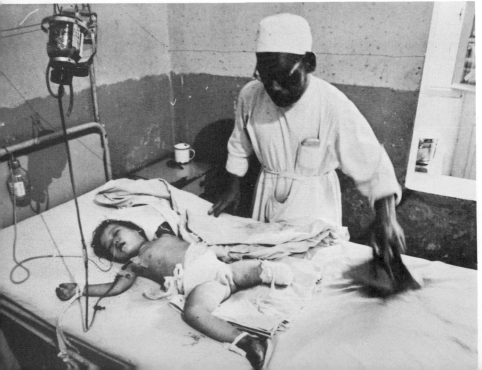

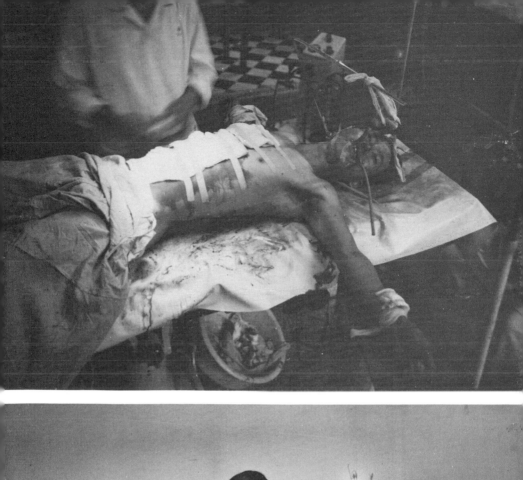
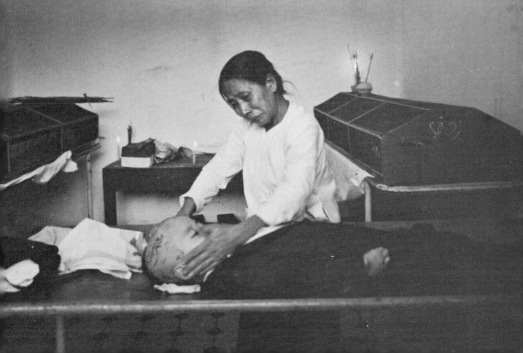

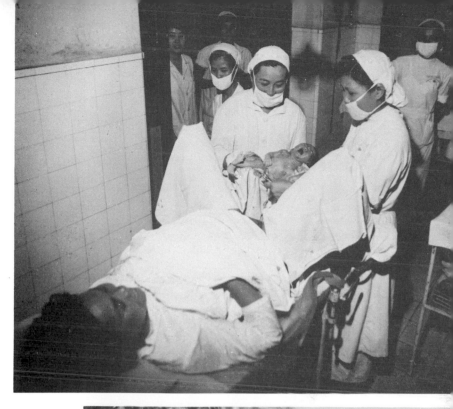

Poems from Vietnam

The Old Mother
To Huu

The old mother stretched on a mat of dry leaves
The old mother unsleeping, restless with sad thoughts...
   Twenty days more, then comes the year's end
The old mother lies there but cannot sleep.

    When will my little youngest son come back to me?
    When he left home it was to join the Liberation
    When will he come back?
    When will there be an end to the enemy
    So that he can come home?

Night after night the mother on the leaf-bed
Softly whispers her prayers.

The old mother stretched out on the bed sleeps not,
The more she thinks the more she is troubled
The more her anger rises and the more she hates.
Outside the bamboo trellis
The great wind of the mountains rises, storming
The night-rain, the rain of the maquis returns
In this night the fighters in the forests, in the dark streams
Are soaked to the bone, hands and feet numb with cold

They go to fight the enemy this night
   The trembling step, the falling step, stumbling, sliding....

    Though we are poor we have a bed of leaves, a fire
to cook rice,
    He goes on such a night as this to fight... and how shall
he be warm?
    In past years we mixed our rice with roots... It was
poor food
    And this year though the rice is good the house is empty
The old mother's heart is torn with worry
Outside from beyond the village the cock crows.
                It is already dawn.

The Highlander

"Man from the mountains, so far from the steep forests of your
                                       ancestral land,
In prison here, say, are you sad?"
The old Highlander, looking into the far blue distance
with eyes sunk in despair
suddenly, with emotion turned,
his heart torn with yearning, in the indifference of evening.
    He looked at me with sorrow and murmured quietly
    "I suffer badly with homesickness..."

So much agony in that word,
drawn out like the yearning of a cricket
crying, lost in the mist of evening.
I hear in silence all his suffering,
his sadness keens in my ear
with the plaint of the high forests.
    So many years away from my woman   me
    and my little children
I suffer so badly with the homesickness."

"And the home-house, and its door
and the suidan-clearing planted with potoato

"And the home-house, and its door
and the suidan-clearing planted with potatoes and with maize,
 and there the great buffalo and the piglets....

To know if all these are still there....
    Or maybe that tiger has come,
    the children and the poor woman left hungry in the mountains."
And suddenly he stops, lost in thought, beaten,
and his mouth opens as though the wind of the
                 far forests of his native mountains
could bring some hint of the scents of home.

And under the shadow of black eyebrows the dusky eyes
like two stony caverns, full of the mists that rise in
                  the mountains at evening

the two eyes darken, absent, they are seeing the
          high forests up home,
there are no tears. I do not know why,
perhaps there are already too many hurtful memories
petrifying the heart into a block of hatred,
hatred of those cruel hands which tore apart and destroyed
the warm nest in the forest by the mountain crest.

Suddenly, like lightning I see the fierce fire of anger
flash in those eyes in the dusk of winter.

The two lips like drawn blades.
    Teeth clenched he murmurs, very low
    "I have such pain in me...Never will I forget that."

And for a long time by the barred threshold of the prison gate
I hear and hear again the voice of the old man speaking.

Crossing the Vam Co River
Giang Nam

At dawn our sampan crosses the Vam Co river
Whose limpid water mirrors rows of coconut trees.
Far is the sea, yet its rhythmic breath is still heard,
And the waves rise and fall like a hammock swinging
                        to and fro.

The ferry girl gently pulls the oar
While the sun's rays and the breeze caress her round
                          arms,
And cheerful songs come from the sugar-cane fields
                    on the banks:
It's Autumn, the season of fighting and of feats of
                      arms.

Life is ours: we rejoice at each market day,
Holding on to our village, to each row of 'mu u'
                    trees,
It took us years of hard life in the jungle, where we
                slept under reed mats,
To be able now to cross the river in broad daylight.

Drinking from the clear river, and living a fighter's life,
How many combatants have you ferried across the
                    river?

How many battles have you fought, younger sister?
Isn't your blouse the colour of a dream?

Leaning my gun against the side of the boat, I offer
                              to row with her.
"Don't trouble yourself, " she says,
Loving freedom, I value all the more the love between
                              fish and water,
With the people, we have everything, earth and skies.
Who has passed by Duc Hoa, and spent the night at
                              Hoa Khanh?
Who has come to Ben Thu, and destroyed the enemy
                              at Go Den?
Loving the Vam Co, I'm grateful to the guerillas
Who have attacked ships and armour, sticking to the
                              ferries and defending the boats...

There lies Duc Tan, with only paddy fields and shade
                              trees,
But there we encircled the enemy with grenades and
                              spike traps.
The enemy "swept" Long Hoa and raided Tan Phuoc,
But our people held on and knocked out a whole
                              regiment!

A thousand wonder stories have become common:
That of the guerilla "expert" who took enemy
                              prisoners,
And of weak-sighted and feeble-legged old mothers
Who have become "addicted" to struggle: marching
                              on the towns, joining in demos.

Oh Vam Co, indomitable river!
Like the Thu Bon and the Mekong,
You have, in twenty years, fought two wars of
                              resistance,
Yet, like them, you remain fresh and strong, and still
                              water hamlets and villages.

Well, my blue-jacketed sister guerilla,
We've arrived. Goodbye, dear sister!
With you, with the liberated zone, in our rear,
I feel the gun firmer in my hand...

                                        August 1964

The Song of the Highland Jungle

We walked on,
   Four days and nights without a stop,
The Truong Son Range was gloomy, desolate
Like lives burdened by sorrow.
The soil crumbled under our feet,
The rain poured down on our heads
Skin yellowing from fever
Eyes dimmed by hunger
That evening, we buried a comrade
On a high hill, where white clouds hovered over the
                        trees.
The enemy was still close around...

We did not weep, yet we felt
The sting in our eyes and salt on our lips.
"You lie here—when victory comes
We will be here again and build a farm
Joining our efforts to yours to settle the new land!"
Then we sprang out into the night,
The cold steel of the guns in our warm hands,
We'll break through enemy lines
To be back among our people.
A lonely star was shining in the dark sky...

The Truong Son Range remained sublime and tranquil,
No one had come and the jungle had not woken up,
Over cold ground, deep pits, cutting grass, thick
                        thorns,
With torn clothes, bare backs lacerated and bleeding,
We marched on...
Some times, stopping at the edge of a stream,
We chew wild leaves and share a pinch of salt
We dreamt of home during troubled slumbers
And of night battles by comrades elsewhere,
Woke up and impatiently waited for dawn.
The jungle was immense and calm as ever,
Hearing monkeys gibber on the boughs
We recalled the cock's crow.
    And this evening
We see footprints on the sandy paths!
Exhausted and giddy, but with joy in our hearts,

We listened to the breath of the jungle...
Theirs or ours? A hamlet or a post?
Oh, how much we long for a warm fire,
A bowl of good soup, a mother's hand
And the sweet smiles of young children!
Here is the hamlet! Blue smoke wreathing up
And buffalo-rattles ringing from afar...
Our feet hesitate, though we want to rush on,
Our lips keep close, though we wish to cry out.
The jungle is going to sleep. The clouds
Seem to float down and stop gliding,
Then rises a song, loud and glowing!
Oh, the song that brings tears to our eyes!
We want to cry and dance and embrace
All—the houses, the hills, the watering-place
The ringing rattles of the buffaloes...
Down the slope we are now rushing,
"Undaunted and lofty highlands..."
That is the call of our own home and people...
And this night, though we hardly know their language
We lie down and listen to the story
Told by old fathers and mothers:
"Years ago, Uncle Ho sent his men here,
We people tilled the land and fought the French
Now we have enough salt and rice
And we shall never forget...
Around the fire, they taught us to read
and to sing songs
About the streams and jungle rains..."
Oh, the same people's hearts, in remote places,
Across hundreds of rivers and brooks,
And we think of old comrades
Who worked behind enemy lines years ago.

Tomorrow we shall go
Mothers carrying rice and fathers leading the way.
Tonight around the warm fire,
We again sit up late and teach the children to sing,
Like the old comrades who came here
To clear the jungle and sow the seeds...

July 1962

Advice to Oneself
Ho Chi Minh

Without the cold and desolation of winter
There could not be the warmth and splendour of
        spring.
Calamity has tempered and hardened me,
And turned my mind into steel.

On the Road

Although they have tightly bound my arms and legs,
All over the mountain I hear the songs of birds,
And the forest is filled with the perfume of spring-
        flowers.
Who can prevent me from freely enjoying these,
Which take from the long journey a little of its lone-
        liness?

The rose at evening blossoms, and then it fades away.
Its opening and its withering continue all unnoticed,
But the fragrance of the rose floats into the depths of
        the prison,
Telling the inmates there of life's injustice and sorrow.

Learning to Play Chess

I

To wear away the time, we learn to play chess.
In thousands, horses and infantry chase each other,
Move quickly into action, in attack or in retreat.
Talent and swift feet gives us the upper hand.

II

Eyes must look far ahead, and thoughts be deeply
    pondered.
Be bold and unremitting in attack.
Give the wrong command, and two chariots are
    rendered useless.
Come the right moment, a pawn can bring you victory.

III

The forces on both sides are equally balanced.
But victory will come only to one side.
Attack, retreat, with unerring strategy:
Then you will merit the title of great commander.

On Reading 'Anthology of a Thousand Poets'

The ancients used to like to sing about natural beauty:
Snow and rivers, moon and wind, mists, mountains,
    and rivers.
Today we should make poems including iron and steel,
And the poet also should know how to lead an attack.

Word Play

People who come out of prison can build up the
    country.
Misfortune is a test of people's fidelity.
Those who protest at injustice are people of true merit.
When the prison-doors are opened, the real dragon
    will fly out.

Peace
Nhat Hanh

They woke me this morning
to tell me my brother had been killed in battle.
Yet in the garden, uncurling moist petals,
a new rose blooms on the bush.
And I am alive, can still breathe the fragrance of roses
and dung,
eat, pray and sleep.
But when can I break my long silence?
When can I speak the unuttered words that are choking me?

M
John Sack

Thursday, Williams, the gentle Florida periscope operator,
achieved immortality of sorts: he really saw a Communist, large
as life and twice as spunky, an experience that no other trooper in
M's alert battalion was to enjoy throughout this Operation.
This special Communist was staring at Williams from a bush no
farther than the other side of a ping-pong table, staring at him
down the gray barrel of a rifle, in fact. *'Ho!'* Williams shouted
in consternation: but to begin at the beginning.

On Thursday, Demirgian's deserving platoon had given
itself a siesta as Williams's company and Morton's company
walked through the dark of Sherwood forest, slow going, all sorts
of tangly things, little red ants, their mission being to destroy
Charlie's source of strength: the Communist stores of rice.
Every time Williams's snail-paced friends came to one they
burned it — two or three tons of this brown river-like stuff could
keep Charlie's battalion marching on its stomach a week, the idea
being. A gay little Vietnamese soldier went along to sanction
any or all burnings or blowings up, first having satisfied himself
that the rice was truly Communist, the soldier having been trained
in this mystic art. Once as their machetes cut through the bushes,
Williams's company came to a stock of Vermont-like maple candy
in laundry-soap sized bars. But being in a cave it just wouldn't
burn. An inventive sergeant began to throw the sugary stuff to
the ants — but no, too time-consuming. Hand grenades? Now he
had maple candy with holes. Nausea-inducing gas? Nothing doing,
it might be against the Geneva convention. At last the patient
sergeant radioed the Army engineers, who blew up the maple
candy with TNT. Bigalow was on this safari in his flack capacity,
a story! he told himself but he couldn't write it, a public information sergeant having told him these predatory doings do not pass
Army censorship. 'You're not going to win friends among
Vietnamese farmers,' Bigalow's sergeant had explained.

Even with machetes, moving in this jungle was like searching
in a big attic closet on a summer morning, old moist bathrobes
drawing across one's face and rusty old clothes hangers snagging
in one's hair, corrugated cardboard beneath one's feet. Further-
more, in this wildwood there were snipers shooting at people,
a rustling in the leaves and a *slap!* But what really bedevilled
Williams's and Morton's companies as they pushed along weren't
their human enemies but ants, little red ants which hadn't seen

juicy Westerners in a quarter century, even the French army hadn't dared go to this treacherous place. Morton would tell himself, *Oh—! here comes another one,* as still another cackling ant threw itself out of the foliage onto his neck, and Morton would roll it off with sweating fingers, his black rifle in his other hand, pressing it to instant death. Morton felt guilty about his extraordinary acts of self-assertiveness; a Baptist, he didn't think God set anything on this earth without having His reason, maybe in little red ants was a liquid to cure malaria, cancer, doctors would find it some day, Morton piously believed. For weeks he would justify his steady slaughter by telling himself, *it didn't make any difference — there were so many of them.* He would remonstrate with Russo, the young desperado of sixteen who swore that if *he* had been in those insect-infested woods that day (he hadn't, he had fainted from the heat) — that *he* would cry, *'Die!'* to every ant he butchered, laughing like Mephistopheles. Morton would smile at Russo tolerantly, saying that all God's ants should be killed with kindness.

Bigalow — now Bigalow was a soldier first, a PIO reporter second, and squeezing his ants between thumb and index finger he mechanically cast their lifeless bodies to the jungle floor. But as Bigalow inched along he also speculated whether there mightn't be a story in them. *How to Kill Ants, by PFC Vaughan A. Bigalow.* He thought. *One way is to throttle your ant by pushing a grain of sand into its throat with a toothpick. A second way . . . .* a microscopic punji pit, a careless ant expiring horribly on a point of a pin. In practice Bigalow killed his ants conventionally: indifferently, paying no mind to their dying agonies while he walked along with the friend who once had twitted him about his ball-point pen. I stabbed! I stabbed! I stabbed! 'Bigalow,' the boy remembered in this incongruous place, 'tell Dubitsky he owes me five dollars.'

'All right,' said Bigalow, slapping a neck-ant.

'And Bigalow. You've got a pair of my khakis.'

'You're right,' said Bigalow, dropping his dead ant down.

'And Bigalow? If the captain doesn't get us out of here, you can have the other pair too.'

But Williams—! It never occurred to Williams's gentle mind to kill these ants: if one of them bit he just brushed it off without taking his grim revenge. And that was Williams's nonbelligerent temper when he had that sudden brush with his Communist, a Vietnamese with a white shirt and *hair*—black hair, Williams would never forget his bushy hair. Resting in a little jungle hole, a gully, hearing a twig crack, turning around, Williams saw this black-haired intruder and shouted, *'Ho,'* ducking into his hole. A bullet burned across his shoulder blade and Williams cried out,

'*Oh,*' burying his startled face in the dirt, holding his rifle high above him like an African's spear, shooting it at the trees one-handed, bang! bang! bang! and crying, '*Sergeant! sergeant! sergeant! come here!*' My kingdom for a periscope!

'What's the matter?' Williams's sergeant called as he hurried to this clamorous scene.

'*Keep shooting!*' Williams shouted while he did exactly that, his face still plowing into the dirt. '*I seed one!*'

'Where?'

'*Out there! He shot me,*' jerking his head up, spying the evergreen trees but no more Communist.

'Whereabouts?'

'*Here—in the shoulder!*'

'Nothing. Maybe a ricochet breezed across it.'

'*Sergeant, that was no ricochet! I'm hit, I know I'm hit!*'

'Rock steady!' said Williams's unruffled sergeant. 'You aren't hit, you've nothing to worry about, you're okay. Rock steady.'

Williams got dazedly to his feet and stared around. He told his sergeant, 'Okay, I'll try.'

'Can you make it through the jungle?'

'I'll try.'

But as Williams resumed his death-march through the tangled vines, the tendrils plucking at his shoulders, pulling at his feet, he feared to see that blackhaired man staring at him from every bush, he imagined the vines to be black hair, black hair to be condensing from the shadowy air. Red ants fell on Williams's sleeve, and Williams duly brushed them off. *I get through this I'm never going back—never!*

His black-haired nemesis or someone else was shooting Americans all of their arduous way through the forest, *slap!* and *slap!* killing two of them, wounding many. Coming to the bright paddies at last, Williams's friends were plenty mad at Communists — believe it! Taking their wild revenge, the irrepressible privates went through a yellow Vietnamese village like Visigoths, like Sherman's army, burning the houses, ripping the clothes, breaking the jars, the rice running out on the muddy floors, '*I won't leave this to the goddam gooks!*' One private shot him a dog, when a sergeant said, '*You're a real good goddam soldier,*' he only laughed. Somebody lit a lighter, '*The lieutenant doesn't want you to,*' '*Fuck the lieutenant,*' the house was in black-tongued flames. Somebody used a grenade launcher, there was nothing left.

The following calm morning, Williams went along the fox-holes to talk to his sergeant and declare himself *hors de combat*. A young-looking boy from the East, Williams's sergeant had earned his reputation for infinite patience as leader of the bowl patrol when the bowl thing happened back on M's cool rubber plantation. Next to each rubber tree was a sort of white cereal bowl, in late afternoon the Vietnamese tree-tappers were to leave it rightside-up to gather rubber or upside down if it threatened rain. But going above and beyond the call of duty, the Vietnamese had always put certain bowls in a third — unauthorized — attitude: tilted, the rubber sap in the moonlight showing the Communist snipers which way to shoot to kill American soldiers best. Evening after evening, Williams's patient sergeant had taken his bowl patrol into the shadowy trees to tilt the white bowls back to proper horticultural angle. Williams could have no more compassionate audience than the saint he was telling today, 'Now, I don't want you to think I'm a comprehentious objector.'

'Do you mean a com-conscientious objective?'

'I don't want you to think I'm one of those. I'll do anything you want me to: exceptin' to kill somebody.'

'Well,' said Williams's sergeant gently. 'Don't you think you're giving up too easy?'

'No, serge, I've tried, I've tried, I've made up my mind. I haven't got it in me to kill, I found that yesterday.'

'Well, there ain't none of us wants to kill somebody. But if it's something got to be done, somebody's got to do it, that's all.'

'Serge, I'm just no use in the jungle unlessin' I can kill someone. I ain't going back to the jungle — I just ain't going back.'

'Well, *somebody* got to go back in that jungle, Charlie ain't coming out,' Williams's patient sergeant concluded.

In the weeks after that at M's sylvan rubber plantation, the soft light slipping through the tall trees, the birds in the leaves, a monkey — the weeks after that, Williams's sergeant made sweet remonstrances, Williams's first sergeant made terrible threats, a courtmartial, six years at hard labor, a dishonourable discharge, but neither the stick nor carrot could change Williams's simple belief, kill or be killed was a law of that jungle and he wanted neither of them. 'The spunkless wonder,' his bitter lieutenant called him at dinner in the officers' tent, thinking, *he's selfish, he's unpatriotic, he says he's scared __ well, so everyone is scared,* and Williams's captain remembered his Goethe class at college, *he only earns his freedom and existence who daily conquers them anew.* Amen to that, the diners in the officers' tent would say, telling themselves, *there's a war on but Williams won't do his part!* The officers had learned to tolerate this in the Vietnamese army, but Williams — he was an American!

An ambulance having been called for, Williams was taken to the rubber plantation's bright landing strip. Then a red-crossed helicopter and a second Army ambulance took him to the dusty, insufferably hot little tent where his division's psychiatrist sat, engrossedly patting a handkerchief on his sweat-soaked arms and elaborately folding it into quarters and sixteenths prior to his sliding it into his pocket. 'Well, Williams? What's your problem?' the psychiatrist began. He was a red-headed captain.

'I don't want no part of this killing people,' Williams replied.

'Now how did this come about?' Distantly the psychiatrist was thinking, *autism — association — ambivalence — affect,* the four signs of schizophrenia they had taught him at Colorado. One of those telltale a's — well, we're none of us perfect. Two of them, uh-oh, three of them, zap! a medical discharge for poor old psychotic Williams.

Williams sat in a chair by the doctor's little desk, the same catty-corner furniture arrangement at which he had once sought work at the VC, the Virginia Carolina Mining Corporation, $1.97 an hour. All that Williams knew of psychiatrists he had acquired on television: he believed that his red-headed doctor would give him some bright-colored blocks to put together in two minutes, schizophrenia he hadn't heard of, three of those *a's* would be gibberish to Williams, *association* might mean the Knights of Pythias or the NAACP, neither of which he had joined. In all innocence he sat in that sweltering tent and answered the doctor's friendly questions. Williams's father had drowned. Williams had had headaches for a month after that. He lived with his mother, but he had a girl. Kathernell was her name. Williams wanted to marry her, and some day he would. Ten minutes later the doctor wrote *'No illness found'* on Williams's mimeographed form and sent him back to his rifle company, where the captain made him a cook instead of a combat soldier and where he learned to mix water, flour, lard, and dark brown gravy base to make gravy.

But back to Friday of the Operation.

Friday the long-awaited happened — M's battalion killed somebody, at last. 'What's the spirit of the bayonet?' those wild-eyed sergeants had cried to M in training, in America. *'To kill!'* M had learned to shout fiercely back. 'The enemy is dedicated — he won't scare away,' old Smoke, its battalion commander, had said to M, eyes aflame. *'You've got to kill him.'* And on Friday morning M inevitably killed, doing its climactic job with mixed feelings, one understands, some of its soldiers queasy in the presence of waxy death, some of them impassive. M had guessed it would be this way — in training camp. Hofelder would think of a Communist running at him savagely, he had asked himself, *could I really kill him?* but a buddy of Hofelder's had simply laughed, saying, 'Shucks, I'm me and he's he,' meaning that if I kill a fellow that is his worry, not mine.

The episode was again the doing of Demirgian's platoon, again it had climbed on those hot APCs and had driven *bump— bounce — bump* to Sherwood forest and beyond, burning more yellow houses as it went. In actual fact, the cavalry's big lieutenant colonel had given his captains the order, *insure that positive identification is made:* a sniper in the house destroy it, otherwise spare it. But through the iteration of imperatives and the abolition of qualifiers and wise apprehension that the colonel couldn't be serious, his order had been almost unrecognizable when it got through channels to Demirgian's Sergeant Gore. Gore had heard the order as, 'Kill everything. Destroy everything. Kill the cows, the pigs, the chickens — *everything.* '

'Well, sir. You can't destroy *everything,* ' Gore had told the glum second lieutenant who relayed this.

'That's what the cavalry said,' the lieutenant had answered unenthusiastically.

'Sir, I won't kill the women and children,' Gore had told him.

But as their APCs rolled by the doomed villages, there were no women or children to be seen, men neither — they'd fled. The burly cavalrymen and Demirgian's platoon had been travelling since 7 — *weird,* Sullivan thought as the morning got hotter, observing that this steel vehicle was always in sunshine, never in shade, although there were scores of white sheepclouds in the blue above him: a Vietnamese weather mystery. But the wonder of wonders was Demirgian. An unaccustomed competence seemed to have stolen across Demirgian's features: his eyes level, his rifle at a steady angle of attack, he reminded one of that paragon of infantrymen that had been painted like a rampant lion on each of their training camp's objets d'art, even on the insides of teacups at the officers' mess. Wednesday had satisfied Demirgian's romantic heart, it had confirmed Demirgian's faith: if he didn't stand in lines but stayed in cavalry columns, if he didn't shoulder a rifle to salute with but to shoot with, ah — then the American army needn't be closed to life's grander moments. Getting into the spirit of his fierce orders, Demirgian shot at a water buffalo and heartily he fired into the yellow haystacks to kindle them. Newman, M's old philosophical alligator trapper, a boy to whom the essence of old country stores, of apple barrels and mackinaws, adhered — Newman climbed from his APC to set fire to one yellow farmhouse, but since he had seen women and children running from it one minute earlier he had serious doubts about the propriety of his task. He said to his sergeant, 'Now, why should I do this? They'll just build another tomorrow,' but really he was thinking, *I burn their farmhouse down, that'll just make them Communists, won't it,* Smoke himself had asserted so. Still,

Newman obeyed his orders, using his Army matches, closing the cover before striking them, the cover inscribed, 'Where liberty is, there is my home — Benjamin Franklin,' the apocalypse drove on.

Then it was that the incident happened. A cavalry sergeant, seeing a sort of bunker place, a hut above, hole below, and hearing some voices inside it, told Demirgian to throw a grenade in. Demirgian hesitating — a soldier we have met before, though not by name, jumped from his APC and flipped in a hand grenade himself. It rolled through the door hitting a sort of earthen baffle before it exploded, and — gasped as ten or a dozen women and children came shrieking out in their crinkled pajamas: no blood, no apparent injuries, though, and — got onto his carrier again, it continued on. The next APC in the column, with Yoshioka aboard, drove up to this hovel, and a Negro specialist-four, his black rifle in his hands, warily extended his head in, peering through the darkness one or two seconds before he cried, *'Oh my God!'*

'What's the matter,' said a second specialist.

'They hit a little girl,' and in his muscular arms the Negro specialist brought out a seven-year-old, long black hair and little earrings, staring eyes — *eyes,* her eyes are what froze themselves onto M's memory, it seemed there was no white to those eyes, nothing but black ellipses like black goldfish. The child's nose was bleeding — there was a hole in the back of her skull.

Needless to say, America hadn't sent M into battle without having taught it the principles of first aid. Sergeants had spun around like T-formation quarterbacks to slap hypothetical wounds into the torso, arms, and legs of talented volunteers, who rolled their eyes to the ceiling in Stanislavskian agonies as their persecutors cried, 'Okay! He is wounded — right? He got a big bad wound — right?' Later in its oral examination of the tenets of first aid, M had been questioned soldier by soldier, 'Somebody's bleeding, tell me the four things you'd do,' and there had been few trainees who couldn't list two or three, at least: [a] elevate the bleeding part, [b] apply a pressure bandage, [c] press on a pressure point, and [d] apply a tourniquet — of course, a tourniquet wouldn't be indicated in the accident today. Nor could it be argued that M was all surgical competence with no human heart, not in the least. If its oral exams had proved anything, it was that M would try to be Nightingales as well as Galens whenever bleeding occurred, many of its tenderhearted boys reciting the Army's four iatrical measures and adding a fifth of their own, 'I'd first make him *real* comfortable,' or 'I'd talk to him . . . I'd talk to him.' Providence had placed the first of those compassionate soldiers at the door to this morning's bunker, but an injury as massive as that staring girl's went far beyond his earnest abilities, and even a PFC medic was saying sadly, 'There's nothing to be done.'

A cavalry sergeant pressed his thumb on the press-to-talk switch of his radio and reported to his captain, 'Sir, there's a little girl, a civilian girl, who is wounded. Can we have a dust-off?' The sergeant hoped for a helicopter to bring the gazing child to one of Vietnam's civilian hospitals, where the patients lie three to a bed with weird afflictions like missing arms and legs and holes in parts of their bodies.

'Roger,' said the cavalry captain, but then the seven-year-old shuddered and died.

'Sir,' said the cavalry sergeant, 'the little girl died.'

'Roger,' said the captain and the APCs moved on, pausing only for specialist number two to give the other children chewing gum and to comfort the girl's mother as best he could, 'We're sorry,' the mother shaking her head embarrassedly as though to say *please — it could happen to anyone,* a piece of shrapnel sticking out of her shoulder; the medic gave her a bandage before he left.

One doesn't doubt, in the many months to come M would see operations with a greater share of glory (and it would see many, the Army would need fifteen hundred operations as vast as this to cover all Charlie's territory, and Charlie might still be back the following evening) — more glorious operations, but this first Operation of M's had come to its melancholy close, and M's tired battalion was to kill, wound, or capture no other Vietnamese, Communist or otherwise, estimated or actual, in the day-and-a-half remaining. Some of M was truly ashamed about the seven-year-old. Sullivan was annoyed with her, *dammit,* he thought, *she should have known we didn't want to hurt her. Why was she hiding out?* Much of M agreed with him, *ignorant people,* they thought. A lieutenant of the cavalry had no misgivings, thinking, *these people don't want us here anyhow, why should I care about them?* a thought that he bitterly volunteered in conversation. In his innocent past, the lieutenant had gone through the empty-looking villages without taking care to destroy them first, a man, a woman, a *boy* opening fire and killing those for whose lives he was responsible. Vietnam had shown to the lieutenant's satisfaction the line where compassion must end, caution begin.

Yoshioka had stood by the bunker watching the girl die. He felt no special affinity towards Asia's troubles, though he was Oriental and his mother had been at Hiroshima, but being an American he did like children — he turned away, his face waxily paralyzed. Life hadn't taught him to phrase his thoughts with any great felicity, and Yoshioka simply told himself his favorite vivid word and promised himself to think of other things. But that he couldn't do, for three Fridays later, jumping from a dusty Army truck, seeing a glistening wire between two bushes, declaring, quite phlegmatically, 'There's a mine,' a sergeant reaching his hand out to keep soldiers back, reaching his hand out, reaching his hand, reaching — three Fridays later in the black explosion Yoshioka was freakishly wounded the same way as that staring child. The sergeant who touched the trip-wire was killed, the Negro who'd found the little girl was killed, M's old alligator trapper, Newman, was ripped in his arms and legs by the whistling pieces of steel and evacuated, and 'Yokasoka's dead,' the soldiers were saying that night at their rubber plantation, still not getting his name right, not knowing how Yoshioka lay in a Saigon hospital vegetally alive, huge Frankenstein stitches on his shaven head, his acne caked with blood, a hole in his throat to breathe through, bubbles between his lips, the soles of his feet a queer pale yellow, his head thrashing right and left as though to cry *no-no-no*, his hand slapping his thigh as though he'd heard some madcap story, a sheet around the bedframe to hold him in — a jar of clear liquid dripping into him, a brownish-yellow liquid dripping out, a PFC shooting the flies away and sucking things out of him with a vacuum machine, a Navaho nurse pulling the sheet up over his legs for modesty's sake, a doctor leaning over him whispering, 'Bob? You're in a hospital. You're going to be on your litter a while. You're going to be travelling some. First you'll be on a plane . . . . '

It chanced that the bed next to Yoshioka's was a crib, inside it a stuffed red polka-dot puppy and a wide-eyed Vietnamese girl of two. Tiny white plaster casts like dinner candles kept her from picking her moist upper lip, where Yoshioka's gentle and good-samaritan doctor had operated to correct a cleft, an ugly defect since her birth.

Saturday, the last scheduled day of the Operation and the fiftieth since the day when Milett had told M, 'I got a wife, three kids at home . . . . ' Saturday, M had nothing to do but push little squares of cotton through its rifle barrels. Demirgian said, 'I cleaned it yesterday,' and with a specialist-four he sat crosslegged on the grass by his foxhole doing the crossword puzzle in *Stars and Stripes*, his curved back to the Communists, if any. 'Appellation of Athena. That's a good one,' Demirgian murmured.

'Room in a harem,' the specialist countered softly.

'Ten down?' Demirgian.

'Nine down,' the specialist.

'Ten down is girl's name is Ann.'

'*Nine* down.'

'Nine down is room in a harem.'

'Like a bedroom?'

'Nine down is what?' Demirgian asked the elements.

Sullivan sat reading *The Unanswered Questions About President Kennedy's Assassination*. Russo was lying down: his beloved bowie knife had vanished in the woods like Excalibur in the lake, he had heat exhaustion besides, and under a coconut tree he whispered his secret age to his friends in arms, hoping they might betray him to the authorities. Morton sat in his foxhole and ate his C-rations, pleasantly he asked his friends about why they burned down the Vietnamese houses — *he* felt funny about it. Friday morning Morton had asked a squad leader, 'Sergeant, should I burn this house?' 'Here, this'll help it,' the sergeant had answered, giving him a jar of kerosene from the kitchen shelf. All right: an order's an order, Morton had accepted that, but then the sergeant had said, 'That's enough,' and Morton's disobedient friends had lazily stayed behind and burned the whole village into a tiny replica of Lidice — now, Morton was good-naturedly wondering why. His friends, all of them old-timers, guaranteed to Morton that he would be less studious of the sensitivities of Vietnamese after a few experiences of their trying to kill him. One of his friends said, 'All these people, the VC come and take their brothers and fathers away, so if they've got family in the VC of course they'll be VC sympathizers.' Another friend said, 'Look at it this way. You burn their house, if they're not a VC now they'll be one after you've burned their house,' by which he meant go ahead and burn it, a tight little circle of reasoning that made even Morton blink. A third of his friends said simply, 'I burn because I hate. I hate Vietnam. I hate it because I'm here. I hate every house, every tree, every pile of straw and when I see it I want to burn it.' He seemed surprised to learn that the rest of Morton's friends had intellectual reasons, as well.

'Well,' said Morton, laughing, 'I guess in a few months I'll be burning houses too!' But that wasn't to happen. For walking down the road two weeks later, there was a noise and Morton died, he was killed by one of Charlie's mines, his legs in the dusty dirt at raggedy-ann angles — Morton seemed to have three or four legs. 'We held divine memorial services in his honor,' the Chaplain wrote to Morton's mother and father in Texas. 'Many were the generous tears as we reflected upon this profound truth, *Greater love hath no man than this, that a man lay down his life for his friends*. It may,' the Chaplain wrote in his standard letter, 'also be of comfort for you to remember that Billy was serving a noble cause, helping good people to live in freedom here and all over the world. You remain in my prayers,' the Chaplain wrote to Morton's parents, who buried him in his one-button suit.

'Site of Taj Mahal,' the specialist-four was saying.

'India! India!' Demirgian cried.

'Too many letters,' the specialist told him. Once they were

through with the puzzle, they turned to the news and discovered a story on the Operation, several days old, on page one.

'Gee,' Demirgian said, 'I didn't think they'd write so much about *this.*'

'*The division,*' the specialist said, reading out loud, '*was in the midst of its biggest campaign of the Vietnam war,* hey I didn't know that, *after pouring thousands of troops into a rugged wooded area . . . .*'

'Wooded!' Sullivan looked up and cried.

'*The battle-hardened division . . . .*'

'Battle-hardened! Ha!'

'*. . . . relying heavily on the element of surprise to catch a huge Vietcong force believed to be holing up in the district, launched its drive with lightning speed at daybreak Monday morning. Troops and tanks, along with armed personnel carriers, have swept into the area to close off the entire circle. Another force of troops is sweeping through the woods to the east . . . .*'

'Caught in the crossfire!' Sullivan cried.

'Whenever the VC duck we shoot each *other,*' the specialist said.

And so M's merriment continued until a sergeant came marching up to this perimeter to tell its defenders to quit goofing off. 'Demirgian! Police up those papers — pick up those C-rations!' And out into no-man's-land Demirgian walked, telling himself that the Army is the Army is the Army . . . but thinking it with a new-found equanimity and getting himself an old C-ration peanut butter lid, a C-ration chicken and noodles can, and an empty carton of Marlboro cigarettes that had been brutally ripped open, and six months later Demirgian was—

Six months later, Sullivan was in Washington in the hospital —*bang,* he had accidentally shot off an inch of his index finger. Yoshioka was in California with a steel plate where his skull had been, and Morton was in Texas with a black carnation in his lapel. Prochaska was on the Riviera on leave, he was dating girls in yellow bikinis. Smith was in Panama a PFC, he had busted out of officer candidate school, *lack of mental adaptability,* and Mason had never become a green beret. A convert to candor, Russo was in Yonkers with his honorable discharge. McCarthy was on a leave in Islip seeing his lawyer and — *stop the presses!* He wasn't in Islip any longer, he was awol, he was over the hill. McCarthy at last was WANTED by the military police — but Demirgian was still in Vietnam. Newman was on the rubber plantation driving a jeep, he was limping and didn't have to fight, and Williams was in the kitchen making a gravy and waiting — waiting — *why doesn't Kathernell write?* Bigalow had re-enlisted till 1970, a bonus of $500. Some of M had medals, a third of M's expeditionary force had been killed or severely wounded, some of M had malaria, M, at times, had been accidentally napalmed or rocketed or shot in the head by sergeants, a second wave of M was upon the waters, Hofelder with it: all aboard to South Vietnam! But Demirgian—

Demirgian was still in his fighting squad, the General had chosen it *best in battalion.* The infantryman *terrible,* terror of sergeants, had himself become an acting sergeant, the leader of five eager privates. While he still had seen no Communists, neither had he met a Vietnamese who cared a fig about Communists or a feather about his fighting them. On operations, Demirgian shot at the pigeons and people's chickens, he stared at the high yellow flames, he found the American army good. Without any shilly-shallying he told his squad, *'I'd like to burn the whole country down and start again with Americans.'* Half of Demirgian's tour of duty was safely over and done.

WORKSHOPS IN GRAPHIC ART
SCULPTURE AND PRINT MAKING

Ken Sprague and Marcia Karp
Holwell Farm East Down
Barnstable
Devon
phone 0271 82 267

What Are We To Do?
Nigel Gray

A Kind of Freedom

Slashed by the blades
of the choppers
the dawn screamed

she watched the flock of leaflets settling
waiting for her man
not knowing his blood was seeping
into the warm earth

instead
came a soldier who mauled her
though she was as cold as the dead

she waited
with the baby at her breast
holding the baby by the hand
while they burned her home
scattered the ashes with a mechanical grab
and landscaped the village
with the craters of bombs

she carried a sack of rice
and the baby on her hip
and the two hens
trussed like suspects for interrogation
and the child led the pig
on a string
and they went in packed trucks
to where the jungle had been pacified
by an aggression of bulldozers

when asked
she repeated
what the loudspeakers repeatedly told her

she had been freed

If Only Presidents Knew Their Nursery Rhymes

The American president was tough
he thought he was big enough
to swallow a fly
people began to die
the president
got indigestion
but he was rough and tough
like the hero of a Western
so he didn't heed no advice
he just demanded further sacrifice
and swallowed a spider
to catch the fly
more people died

but the spider
was worse than the fly
so ignoring the cries
that he must have heard
he swallowed a bird
to catch the spider
he swallowed to catch the fly
and more people died
and the president lied
through his teeth
as he laid the'wreath
and he said
how he mourned the dead
but the bird was still flapping
so he swallowed a cat
to deal with the bird
and the spider and the fly
still more people died
and he thought that was that
but the cat clawed his guts
so in a terrible rage
but with a smile on his face
from the TV station
he informed the nation
his health was fine
but to deal with the mog

he needed a dog
starred and striped and tough
that was trained well enough
to withstand the draft
and the little dog laughed
to see such fun
wagged its tail and went
to sort out the cat and the bird and the spider
that had already been sent
to take care of the fly
and still more people died
and the President said
with his face rather red
he was practically cured
but his stomach looked bloated
and continued to swell
and he didn't look well
and the rumour spread
that he'd soon be dead
so in desperation
after quick castration
with a wave of the flag
he got a goat in the bag
to deal with the turmoil
he suffered inside
and more people cried
but he refused to hear
he blocked his ears
and said with a smile
to the men from the press
that he'd hazard a guess
in no time at all
he'd be well
and what the hell
if some livestock was lost
you can't count the cost
in such a case
because the loss of face
of the American president
would be too big a disgrace

but to the President's horror
the goat was a failure
though it did its best
to deal with the rest
including the fly

and the world heard the cry
from the President's bowels
and some blocked their ears
to the screams and the howls
but others asked why
people continued to die
but he wouldn't listen to reason
he called it treason
to oppose his will
he had the jails filled
and ordered the cops
to deal with any who dared
to protest at his decisions
so those who cared
found themselves in prisons
or in hospital beds
with broken heads
but they still asked why
the President added lie onto lie
and the innocent victims
continued to cry
and to die
and the fly
that the President thought
he could swallow
was still alive
continued to wallow and thrive
while he thought only of force
and called for a horse
to settle the trouble that was caused by the fly
more and more people died
the President claimed he was strong
there was nothing much wrong
but we knew it was a lie
our sight was scraped by the dying
our ears clawed by the crying
our brains ripped by the lying
and as things got worse
we prayed for the day
they'd call for the President's hearse

For a Girl Who Stopped Growing
After Being Napalmed

We undressed you
stood and stared
in a gaping circle
we took photographs and film
to display you to the world
in your nakedness
your innocence
left undesired
unwanted
because you will be
a little girl
for ever
and who could violate
a child
who has been so violated
raped by the rockets of war
burnt with the fire of hate
beauty turned into ugliness
as you turned your back
they turned to fláme
the flesh of a child
on the threshold of love
on the threshold forever
of womanhood
of motherhood
loveless and childless
for who could caress
your skin like lava
from the erupted volcano of war
your petrified molten skin
wasted
wasted years
and wasted love
for how could you feed
your child
when the milk has dried up
before your breasts have formed
and the pity of it all
is the pity

you will be given
in place of the love
of the family
that died in the fire
and you are the ashes
the evidence of the arson
the proof of the crime
the exhibit on display
to display their guilt
to the world
and so we make you a thing
and in the name of humanity
take away your humanity
with your dress
and we stand and stare
in a gaping circle
and you
poor little deflowered virgin
turn your eyes to the ground
till we turn our backs
to clamour for facts
and then go away
but your pain
will remain
for the brief eternity of your corrupted youth

What Did You Feel?

What did you feel
on the day the war ended
what did you feel
when Saigon fell

       cash down the drain
       said the Chicago banker
       I made it alive
       said the grunt on the plane

what did you wish for
on the day the war ended
what did you wish for
when Saigon fell

       my husband to share it
       said the young widow
       my legs said the invalid
       my legs back again

what did you say
on the day the war ended
what did you say when
when Saigon fell

       where are my children
       said the blind mother
       there's work to do
       said the war-weary man

what did you do
on the day the war ended
what did you do
when Saigon fell

       I sat down and cried
       said the torture victim
       I danced said the soldier
       though my legs were like lead

where will you go
now the war's ended
where will you go
now Vietnam's free

       we'll walk into the future
       said the children
       I'll go back home
       said the refugee

Aftermath

I feel I need to apologise
for mentioning Vietnam
I could be accused of
disturbing the peace
the war is over
there's nothing more to be said
we would like to wipe away the memory
like a rude picture
cleaned from the blackboard
with one movement of the hand

but I wonder what it's like
not to have legs

dioxin
a by-product of chemical defoliant
has been absorbed by rice and fish
the food of the people
it causes cancer of the liver

I won't list the atrocities
that would be like
reading the names from the telephone directory
to illustrate how many of us
don't want to know

but you
who argued against the war
as well as those
who turned a blind eye
know that the deaf child
hears your coins jangle on the pub counter
the burnt survivor
winces as the blue smoke rises
from the burning cigarette
and the mutilated
itch in their nerve endings
when you run
to work or at play

during the war
we asked
        WHAT ARE WE TO DO?

now the war is over
the question remains